Action Unlimited:

The Band of Gold

Action Unlimited:

The Band of Gold

A Kentucky Band's Musical Journey to the Edge of Stardom

By Dewey Pope

Acclaim Press
MORLEY, MISSOURI

Acclaim Press
— Your Next Great Book —
P.O. Box 238
Morley, MO 63767
(573) 472-9800
www.acclaimpress.com

Editor: Charles A. Francis
Book Design: Rodney Atchley
Cover Design: M. Frene Melton

ISBN: 978-1-942613-73-2 | 1-942613-73-3
Library of Congress Control Number: 2017911037

First Printing: 2017
Printed in the United States of America
10 9 8 7 6 5 4 3 2 1

This publication was produced using available information.
The publisher regrets it cannot assume responsibility for errors or omissions.

Contents

Acknowledgments 6
Foreword by Randy Westbrook 8
Prologue 10

Chapter One: The Beginning 13
Chapter Two: Speck's and The Monzzas 19
Chapter Three: Action Unlimited–The Beginning 27
Chapter Four: Prepping to go to California–Winter 1965 35
Chapter Five: The Adventure Begins–February 1966 39
Chapter Six: California 47
Chapter Seven: Thunderbird Hotel–Las Vegas 53
Chapter Eight: The Tour 59
Chapter Nine: Sacramento, CA–Hilton Inn–San Francisco 65
Chapter Ten: The Carousel Club–Oxnard, California 69
Chapter Eleven: Seaside, Oxnard and Back to Vegas 75
Chapter Twelve: Recording First Record 81
Chapter Thirteen: Drum Lessons, Draft Boards and Portland 87
Chapter Fourteen: Back to Fresno–
Shindig!–San Francisco–Utah 95
Chapter Fifteen: Palm Springs, California 133
Chapter Sixteen: Back to Portland 139
Chapter Seventeen: Christmas in Kentucky,
Then Back to Portland 145
Chapter Eighteen: Back to Hollywood–
Our Second Recording Session, and Palm Springs Again 149
Chapter Nineteen: Chuk Leaves AU, Followed by Jon 153
Chapter Twenty: Kent, Then I Leave the Band 157

Epilogue 161
Afterword 163
About the Author 172
Index 173

Acknowledgments

There are several people that deserve recognition for the writing of this book. I echo my good friend Rick Lee, the author of *Tribute to Valor and Courage* who stated, “No worthwhile endeavor is ever accomplished in singularity.” I didn’t take this journey by myself. I am simply the storyteller of a remarkable group of musicians who shared the adventure of a lifetime with me. It took 50 years and I owe many thanks to all listed below in helping me to tell the story of a remarkable journey.

I have to first thank my mother who cashed one of her valued insurance checks to buy my first set of drums and believed in me from the very beginning. My father weathered through many nights of me practicing and ultimately was one of my biggest supporters.

I want to thank my wife and partner Anne for her love, encouragement and support for the last 44 years. She spent many nights at home with our children while I was off playing, never once complaining, and often accompanying me on band gigs. I thank my three children, Jamie, Julie and Beth for all their support as well especially in proofing the manuscript text and encouraging me along the way.

Rick Lee (the above mentioned author) was a great inspiration by giving me such a great example to follow. I consulted with him many times for advice and counsel on the process of writing a book. George Ridings, one of the original drummers of the Maroons provided valuable pictures and information on the beginnings of the Maroons (which later became Action Unlimited) especially through the Gary Edwards years. I couldn’t have accomplished the project without the help of Jon Anderson, Chuk Trisko and Kent Fox, who supplied a treasure trove of pictures, anecdotes and facts that were very essential in the foundation and structure of the book. All of us in the group, and our families, have Dave Osborne and Sam McIntosh in our thoughts and prayers as they both have had serious health problems the last few years. Sam's wife, Lisa, and Dave's wife, Jeanne, kept me up to date on both of them and their recovery progress. Jeanne, and her daughter Dawn, provided encouragement and support for the book as well as helping to put together our Action Unlimited reunion in 2003.

To Bud Ecton, my hero and early mentor, thank you for having the patience to take the time to show a young kid how to be a drummer. You still are the best.

Thanks to Paul Martin and Kent Slucher for putting Winchester, Kentucky on the map for all future young musicians to aspire to. You make us proud.

To Randy Westbrook, thanks for writing the Foreword to this book. Randy authored the book *50 Years of Exile*, an outstanding history of Exile, a band whose early members we got to know well during our days at Speck's in Richmond. I was honored that you took the time to pen a Foreword that captured the essence of the Action Unlimited story.

Thanks to Doug Sikes and Charlie Francis at Acclaim Press. Doug (publisher), for believing in me from the beginning to make this book happen, and Charlie (editor) for all his expertise throughout the editing process. I am forever grateful to both.

And finally, to all my family, friends, and musicians who encouraged me over the years to write this story, I thank you from the bottom of my heart. It was a journey that I will cherish and remember—a story worth telling.

Foreword

By Randy Westbrook

The history of rock 'n' roll has provided a seemingly endless supply of intriguing stories. Those interested in popular music often enjoy learning about behind-the scenes figures, songwriters, session players, and musical movements. That's why books such as this are important. They give the reader a glimpse into the realities that surround the music business. As a musician and educator who works consistently in local venues and institutions in the central Kentucky area, I value the various connections that I feel with the artists who helped to develop a music scene in the region. As the author of the book *50 Years of Exile: The Story of a Band in Transition,* I was able to explore the history of one of central Kentucky's most influential bands. The history of Exile led me in various directions as I talked with many of the musicians involved with the band's history. In the process of conducting the interviews I learned about the various projects that current and former members of the band had been involved with over the years. These interviews helped to emphasize the fact that Exile did not exist in a vacuum, despite their many achievements. The history of rock, soul, and pop music in central Kentucky is diverse and complex. The stories that Dewey Pope presents in this book provide key insight concerning the history of popular music in central Kentucky, and it also includes detailed information about Action Unlimited's experiences in Los Angeles and other areas on the west coast during an era that was pivotal in the history of rock music.

Dewey and Action Unlimited looked to find success in the music business at a time that seems distant and unimaginable today. After The Beatles performed on *The Ed Sullivan Show* in 1964, rock 'n' roll bands began to form throughout the United States. They were formed by musicians who were influenced by early rock 'n' roll, soul music, and blues-based records that were released by British bands. Groups such as The Maroons and Action Unlimited played consistently during that time, and they helped to bring a new musical consciousness to Richmond, Kentucky and those attending Eastern Kentucky University. Action Unlimited was the first rock group from Richmond that was invited to Los Angeles by those associated with Dick Clark Productions, and they were also the first to record a single on a major label ("My Heart Cries Out"/"Thinking to Myself"). Like other groups from this period, their dream was cut short by various external circumstances, but their place in the history of the central Kentucky music scene was already established. Dewey's book works to document his experiences with Action Unlimited, but it also serves as a welcome addition to a growing number of publications related to a time that continues to be a source of great memories for many who were attending shows during the mid-1960s. The building that was at various points called Speck's, The Steak Out, and The Family Dog is no longer in operation, but its presence serves as a reminder that the sound of groups such as Action Unlimited, The Maroons, and The Exiles once provided the sonic blueprint for the music scene in Richmond, KY.

For some, this book will bring back memories. For others, it will provide an account of what it was like for bands in the 1960s when classic rock formats had yet to fully develop and artists were dependent upon LPs and concerts to market their music. The bands in the 1960s generally weren't formed in studios. They had to pay their dues on the road, and this included many long stints at various clubs. The life of an aspiring rock musician was difficult, but the possibilities seemed endless. Action Unlimited recorded their only single during the year in which The Beatles' *Revolver*, The Beach Boys' *Pet Sounds*, and The Mothers of Invention's *Freak Out!* were released. Rock was moving in various experimental directions at a rapid rate.

Perhaps the strongest point of this book is its emphasis on the rock 'n' roll dream and the ways in which various members of the band were affected by it. In the pre-Internet, pre-cable, pre-downloading, pre-cell phone world of the 1960s, the mythology surrounding rock 'n' roll was much more mysterious. Listeners had to buy albums and go to shows in order to hear some of the music. A show called *The Monkees* depicting a fictional rock band originally aired from 1966-1968, and many viewers envisioned a time in which they could move west to chase the dream of rock stardom. Dewey and his band mates had the courage to pack up and make the trip from Kentucky to Los Angeles, and the stories in this book are more intriguing than the writers for any television show could hope to come up with.

Well, that's enough from me. Sit back and remember a time when so many things were new. Let the journey begin.

Prologue

1957

It all started on a normal day in the sixth grade at Hickman Street Elementary, located in Winchester, Kentucky. Hickman Street Elementary was composed of the main building and a one-story gym in the left rear. The school was very old, even at that time, and had large columns at the front entrance and two stories with a cavernous basement that also housed the cafeteria. There were bicycle racks to the front left for all of us who rode our bikes each day. The cafeteria, which was located in the basement, had a low ceiling with rock walls and tables with bench seats.

For the first five years, during my eight years there, I experienced the normal routine of grade school life, but on this particular day in the sixth grade, I remember we were called out to the gym for an assembly. The gym was a one-story building with an asphalt roof and shingle siding. The interior had a wraparound balcony, with a stage on one end and a typical basketball court floor with bleachers on both sides. For the most part, I wasn't in the gym much, as I didn't play sports (too little for basketball and too small for football) and was only in there for special assemblies and other events.

After filing in and being seated, I noticed a drum on a stand sitting out on the gym floor along with some other instruments. At the time, I didn't know that this was a snare drum, but I remember it had a bright colorful finish and I couldn't take my eyes off of it. After we were all seated and started our usual loud sixth grade conversations, one of the teachers came onto the floor and, of course, quieted us promptly. He then introduced himself as a music teacher and mentioned that he was recruiting music students for eventual positions in the junior high school band. I still couldn't take my eyes off the drum until I heard him say that they especially needed drummers and invited anyone interested to come down for a closer look at the instruments. I was the first one down to the snare drum, and I knew then, on that day, that I wanted to be a drummer.

The music teacher went on to explain the process of becoming a band member and then came the ultimate commitment—the price of the instruments. Naturally, they were not free. There was a cost, and he even offered a payment plan, which I was very excited about and couldn't wait to get home and tell my parents about. I don't remember the exact cost of the snare drum, maybe $60.00, but for my family and me, that was a fortune. After the assembly, I could not concentrate on anything for the rest of the day, especially schoolwork. All I could think about was playing that snare drum in the school band and maybe someday becoming a professional drummer.

When I got home and relayed to my parents the exciting experience that day at school, they were supportive and wanted me to pursue this wonderful venture. Then, my father asked me if the school furnished the drum or if I had to buy it. When I mentioned the price, he looked at me very sadly and said the most disheartening words, which I still remember vividly, "Son, we can't afford it." I explained the payment plan, and it still didn't solve the financial problem that the extra money would cause.

The next day was hard for me because I saw several of my classmates sign up for not only drums but also the other instruments. One of my close friends signed up for the drums, and it broke my heart because I wanted to be there with him. (I have to mention that he went on to become a fine snare drummer throughout high school and still plays as a professional drummer today.) I had always been interested in art and displayed a high aptitude for it, so from that point on until later years, I concentrated on art, hoping to get my mind off that drum and being a musician. Little did I know that, just a few years later, I would become a professional musician and take a journey that would mark my life for years to come. This is that story.

Chapter One

The Beginning

I want to include this part of my early years on the drums, as it plays an important part in my eventually becoming the drummer for Action Unlimited. After being so disheartened during the sixth grade and not being able to follow my dream to become a drummer in the school band, I did concentrate on art and actually did quite well. But I still had the burning desire to become a drummer. During my sophomore year of high school, especially the summer before, I would listen just to the drums on any song I heard and also paid a lot of attention to one of the finest drummers to come out of my hometown, Bud Ecton. Bud was the drum major for the high school band and played the drum kit during halftimes for the school football games. He also played with a band for the school "sock hops," and I would stand behind him, or as close as I could get to him, and watch every move he made. I don't think he realized that I was so engrossed with his playing, but he did later become a mentor and gave me some of the best impromptu lessons and tips I ever received as a drummer.

During the summer between my sophomore and junior year of high school (1962) my mother bought me my first snare drum from Sears, Roebuck and Co. It was the standard size, 14 inches, with a blue sparkle finish and snare stand, 10-inch cymbal and sticks. It cost $29.95, but to me, even though it wasn't an expensive drum, it was that snare that I wanted back in 1957. It was perfect, and I started to work immediately trying to learn how to play it. At that time, I didn't know how to read music, as I had not had any lessons, so I started training myself to play by ear. Whatever I heard, I tried to emulate it, of course making lots of mistakes and creating bad habits. I didn't care as I had a drum and was on my way to becoming a drummer, finally.

On Saturday nights, Lawrence Welk would be on TV and I would set my drum (and cymbal) up and try to play along, watching Johnny Cline,

Lawrence Welk's drummer at that time. I had to use brushes because my father went to bed early, and with us living in an apartment, the sound carried with the sticks and he would get upset with me for interrupting his sleep. So, I used the brushes and did my best to keep up with Cline and play quietly enough to not wake up my father. I was still keeping up with Bud and his bands, as he had already graduated from high school, and went to see him play every chance I got, still watching and learning.

I did the Lawrence Welk thing for the fall and winter of 1962 and also spent a lot of time at a friend's house listening to every record I could, trying to learn the drum beats and grooves, as I didn't have a record player. One record that I remember specifically was "Walk Don't Run." I was really taken with the drums on it and think that was probably the first true groove that I learned and later used a lot.

I also started taking drum lessons from Cecil Jones in early 1963 on a weekly basis, and he straightened out a lot of my bad habits and gave me my first exposure to reading music and learning drum rudiments. I will always remember him asking me to do a press roll for him. I did, and he wasn't too impressed. He then told me to practice it continuously until I could make it sound like "running water." I was using the traditional grip then, and he taught me the right way to grip the left stick, setting up a whole new set of blisters, but it really improved my sticking.

But all during this time, I did not have a set or kit of drums yet. I was still playing my single snare drum along with the small cymbal, and that was it. In the spring of 1963, I met Kent Fox and C.B. Spicer. They were two musicians, also in the school band, who had a small rock group that I thought a lot of. They would practice in the band room of the high school in the afternoons after school, and I would always try to be there to watch and, again, learn. Their drummer, Bill Joyce, eventually left, and they were holding tryouts for a new drummer. Well, after taking drum lessons and being full of confidence that I could do the job, I decided to try out. I still didn't have a kit, so I showed up to the audition with my snare drum and single cymbal. At one point, Kent asked me where the rest of my kit was, and I had to explain that I didn't have any more to set up, just the snare and cymbal. We proceeded with the audition and I obviously didn't do well, especially not having a kit to play. After a few songs, the audition was concluded and I got the famous, "don't call us, we'll call you." They didn't call, and I knew that I had to get a kit and learn a lot more, as just being a snare drummer would not cut it in a rock band. I was hurt and my confidence blown to bits, but I didn't give up.

I had a family friend, Paul Wasson I had known for many years but hadn't realized that he played bass until the spring of '63. He had a good friend, Jimmy Thomas, who was a guitar player, and they both saw something in my drumming and asked me to play with them. Again, I didn't have a drum set, so I actually used a cardboard box for a bass drum, pots and pans for toms, and probably generated the most unusual sound for drums ever created.

During the early summer of 1963, Paul, Jimmy and I met at Paul's house and practiced. We practiced for a few weeks and then a miracle of sorts happened in July of 1963. I saw an advertisement for a used drum set in the newspaper, a set of Ludwig white pearl drums for $165.00. The set consisted of a bass drum, snare (with stand), mounted tom and a couple of cymbals with stands.

Of course, $165.00 was a lot of money, and I had no way to come up with it quickly before someone else bought them. I had a paper route at the time, but my weekly salary was about $7.00, and that didn't help in the short run. By chance, I mentioned it to my mother, and she assured me that she had an idea that might work. My parents had taken insurance policies out on me when I was very young, and one of them had matured and had a cash-in value. She contacted the company, cashed in the policy and went with me to look at the drums, knowing we were going to buy them. A fellow named W.A. Smith owned the drums. My mom called a cab to take us there and had the cab driver wait outside while we went in. Mr. Smith took us up to the attic, and there they were. It was the most beautiful set of drums that I had ever seen—in mint condition! We bought them on

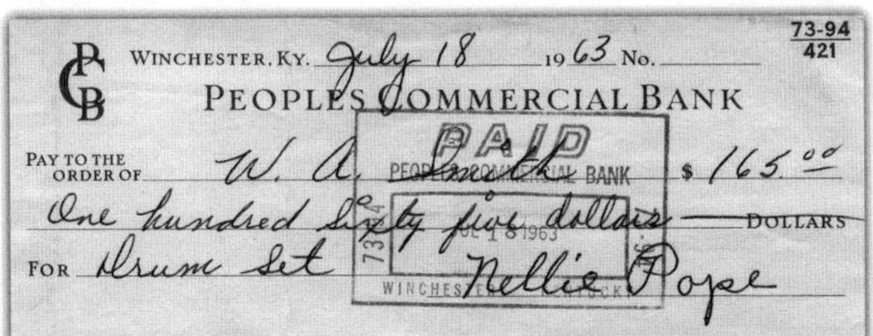

The check that paid for my first real drum kit

the spot, loaded them into the cab and headed home. That was one of the happiest days of my life.

So, now I had a set of drums. Paul and Jimmy had some friends who wanted to hire us to play for their family reunion picnic. I did not have a lot of time to practice, so we played the picnic, with me performing on a real set of drums for the first time on my first job. I was proud and

My first group at the Silo Club in Winchester, Kentucky. Glen Rogers (guitar), Philip Abney (singer), Paul Wasson, (guitar), Dewey Pope (drums) and Jimmy Thomas (guitar).

confident, though I had no idea how bad I must have sounded. But it didn't matter. I was finally a drummer with a band.

We continued to practice and picked up another guitar player, Glen Rogers, and a singer, Phillip Abney. We started to get gigs at a couple of Winchester's local bars during the latter part of that summer. I was so young that, when we took breaks, the club owners would make me go back to the storage room because they did not want to get caught with underage kids in their establishment.

Somehow we were hired to play for an outside event for one of the electrical company picnics and as we were playing, I noticed some people watching me from behind the stage. On the next break, Kent Fox and C.B. Spicer came down and complimented me on how much I had improved and offered me a job in a new band they were starting. Now, these were the two guys that I had auditioned for a few months earlier who I hadn't heard from, but now I was thrilled that they wanted me as their drummer. But I also felt a great sense of loyalty to Paul and Jimmy, as they had given me my first job and we had worked hard together and were getting better all the time. It would be a hard decision.

I talked to both Paul and Jimmy in depth about it. They were very supportive and encouraged me to take the job. Actually, Kent and C.B. liked Paul's playing as well and offered him the job of bass player in the new band. Jimmy wanted to stay with Glen, Phillip and the other guys, so Paul and I left. I had no idea where this new move was going to go, but somehow I knew it was the right thing to do. I was on my way.

Chapter Two

Speck's and The Monzzas

The new group, starting out with Kent Fox (guitar), C.B. Spicer (saxophone), Danny Ritchie (guitar), Paul Wasson (bass guitar), Gary Spencer (singer) and me on drums, was a big jump. We had a few practices but didn't have a name for the group. I remember we had a meeting to come up with a name and, after much deliberation, we came up with The Monzzas. The Monza was a new car that had just come out from Chevrolet. We all liked the name but were concerned about copyright infringement, so we added an extra "Z" to keep it legal for us.

Danny Ritchie left the group after a short while and Kent became the lead guitar player. In the fall of 1963, we were playing school dances and fraternity parties and becoming more and more popular. We eventually started practicing in downtown Winchester at Kent's father's photography studio, which was on the second floor across from the courthouse and over a bank. In the summertime, not having air conditioning, we would open the windows and anyone walking, or driving, on Main Street could hear the music. The local newspaper did a short piece on us, calling it "Hidden Music." The article described the music as follows:

"Hidden Music"; Motorists and other passers-by were entertained with band music as they drove along Main Street in Winchester tonight but could not find the source of the music. Several cars stopped and their occupants discovered that the "Monzza band", a group of Clark County teenagers, had just moved into new quarters in the Wiggins Building and were conducting their first practice. Motorists said lights were on in the rear of the building but they could not be seen from Main Street." (*Winchester Sun*, October 10, 1963)

By this time, I was a senior in high school and devoting all my spare time to the group. Gary Spencer and Paul Wasson eventually left the group and Kent took over the bass guitar position, leaving the lead guitar slot open. We hired Tommy Wilson, from Lexington, to take over the lead guitar slot and also added Larry Weisinger, a close friend of Tommy's from Lexington, to fill out the group as a rhythm guitarist. Tommy had just gotten back from being on the road throughout the West Coast, and he added very valuable experience and leadership to the group. Larry played rhythm for a while then, eventually, became our first keyboardist. Kent, C.B. and I became very close friends during our time in the Monzzas and still are to this day. We became so popular in Winchester and the central Kentucky area that there was a Monzza Fan Club created by friends of the band that, in a short time, had a sizeable membership.

Needing a way to transport equipment, I bought a 1955 Chevrolet station wagon, and we used that to carry our band equipment from job to job. After my station wagon broke down, we transported our equipment in C.B.'s VW station wagon. I remember one particular trip that we were making to Berea, Kentucky to play a job when we had an accident, taking down a considerable amount of fence line on a two-lane road, ending up in a field amongst several cattle. There was a lot of damage to the front end, but the vehicle could still be driven. C.B. somehow backed it out of the field and back onto the road, and we drove on to Berea. It was daylight when we wrecked, so we didn't need lights to drive, but on the way home that night both headlights were shining straight up into the air. Needless to say, it was very hard to see the road, but we made it home safely.

We also cut our first record as a backup band for a local Lexington musician by the name of Ronnie Hilliard. We met him when he was with a Lexington group named Ronnie and the Sensations. Ronnie took on the name Pepper Swift and asked us to back him on his record. We did and the record made it into the top 20 in the local market. Ronnie went on to become quite successful in Nashville in later years.

Denny Mitchell, a Lexington deejay for the WLAP radio station, eventually noticed us and became our manager. Denny had a very popular radio program called "Denny's Den" on every night, and he would interview us on the program, which helped our popularity in the central Kentucky area tremendously. He would show up at our jobs in a very unique way, calling ahead to tell us he was coming, somehow talking the local police into giving him a police escort, showing up with sirens and flashing lights. Everyone was impressed, and it made us look like we were very important to have a manager with a police escort.

Sometime during the spring of '64, we got a job at Speck's in Richmond, Kentucky. Speck's was a college club, a sort of melting pot for all the local groups in the central Kentucky area. The club, in downtown Richmond, especially catered to the students from Eastern Kentucky University with standing-room-only crowds from Wednesday through Saturday nights. Playing at Speck's was a big boost for us as it was one of the most popular clubs in the area, and it gave us wide recognition with the diverse student crowds from all over the state. We did the job, were asked back and eventually played there on a regular basis. Two other bands playing there a lot were The Exiles and The Maroons. We became close friends with members of both groups. We were always well received at Speck's and enjoyed playing there tremendously.

The Monzzas eventually ended up playing in a tri-state area of Kentucky, Ohio and Indiana through Denny's management. Throughout 1964 and '65, the group continued playing at Speck's and several Lexington clubs including The Palms and The Terrace Room, all very popular clubs at that time.

In the spring of 1965, Kent left to become the bass player for the Maroons, and it was never the same for me after he left. The Monzzas replaced Kent with Tommy Wilson's brother, Ronnie Wilson, and we continued on through the summer of 1965. C.B. and I left the group

The Monzzas playing at George Rogers Clark High School in 1965.

Right: The record "Fun" made by Ronnie Hilliard aka Pepper Swift and The Monzzas on the WVLK chart for the week of March 10, 1965.

Below: The record that The Monzzas made with Ronnie Hilliard, aka Pepper Swift, entitled "Fun." This was the first record that any of us had ever performed on and was cut at Whirlaway Studios in Lexington, Kentucky.

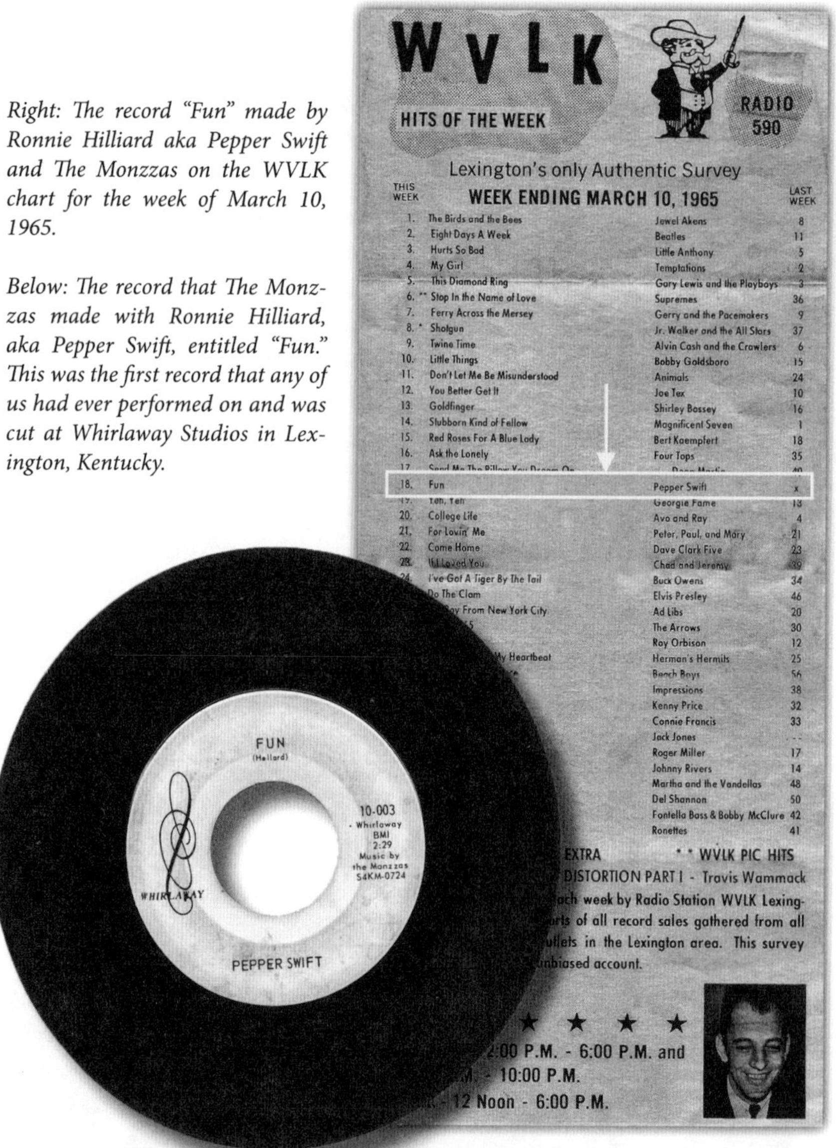

together at the end of that summer. C.B. went on to play with a group named Superband and several other very popular groups in the area. He had developed a reputation as a really good saxophone player and was in demand by lots of groups in the area.

The Monzzas were very popular and well followed in the central Kentucky area and continued on after Kent, C.B. and I left. They eventually broke up in late '65 and Tommy Wilson went on the road with the national group, The Drifters, as the lead guitar in their backup band. Ronnie and Larry continued to play in the Lexington area. Tommy and Ronnie have both since passed away and Larry still lives in Lexington. Kent, C.B. and I are all three still playing some 50 years later.

One of the groups mentioned before in the Speck's lineup was The Exiles. The group was formed in the early '60s and was playing in the Richmond and central Kentucky area when we met them at Speck's in 1964. The group was then composed of Jimmy Stokley (lead singer),

Speck's in downtown Richmond, Kentucky (www.Speck'sEKUAlumni.com)

The Speck's crowd. (www.Speck'sEKUAlumni.com)

The group's first single was released in April, 1962, "Someday I'll Be The One/ Don't Leave Me Baby, Don't" on the Queen label. The Maroons had one other single in 1963, "At The End Of Each Day/Just Checkin" on Jimbo Label. (http://whitedoowopcollector.blogspot.com/2010/01/maroonsdont-leave-me-babydont.html)

Mike Howard (lead guitar), Paul Smith (bass/guitar), Mack Davenport (drums), Billy Luxon (trumpet), J.P. Pennington (bass) and Buzz Cornelison (keyboards).

I became good friends with Mack, who was a fine drummer, and we always enjoyed seeing each other and talking drums. The band and I would always go see The Exiles on our nights off, especially when they were at Speck's, because they were very good and entertaining. Jimmy Stokley was a showman on stage through and through.

Mike Howard left the group in the late '60s because of the military draft and went on to serve in Vietnam. Jimmy Stokley and Paul Smith are both deceased. J.P. is the only one left in the current group from the 1963-66 era. None of us had any idea, at that time, that they would end up becoming a major national act with a classic number

The Maroons, with Gary Edwards, on stage at Speck's. (www.Speck'sEKUAlumni.com)

one hit, "Kiss You All Over," in 1978, 10 number one hits in later years, and an eventual induction into the Kentucky Music Hall of Fame. Now known simply as Exile, they became one of the best bands to ever come out of Kentucky. They are still performing and touring nationwide.

The Maroons were founded in 1961 by Chuck Campbell, who was a student at Eastern Kentucky State College (later known as Eastern Kentucky University). Chuck started out as the drummer but eventually became a singer and leader of the group. George Ridings took over the drumming duties from Chuck, and the original group was composed of Chuck (singer), George (drums), Larry Joe True (bass guitar), Ray Linville (guitar), Jimmy "Hutch" Hutcherson (vocals), John Moore (trumpet) and Bob Becker (sax). Chuck, Ray, John, and Bob eventually left the group. The group then added Bill Rauth (lead guitar), Dave Osborn (singer/trumpet), Tom Colgan (keyboards), Jon Anderson (singer/saxophone) and Gary Edwards (lead singer).

The group was originally named The Impressions before deciding on The Maroons, which tied in with the college colors. The Maroons played many venues around the state, including the Queen's Ball at the Kentucky Mountain Laurel Festival (which had touted such talent as The Glenn Miller Orchestra and Ray Anthony Orchestra); The Golden Horseshoe and Club 68 in Lebanon, Kentucky; University of Kentucky

The Maroons, 1965. L-R: Tom Colgan, Jon Anderson, Bill Rauth, Dave Osborn, Phil Slusher and Pete Stoner. (www.Speck'sEKUAlumni.com)

Fraternity parties and high school proms and dances. They eventually found their way to Speck's located in downtown Richmond and became one of the most popular groups to play there.

Upon graduating from EKU in May of 1964, George Ridings, Gary Edwards and Larry Joe True left the group. Phil Slusher replaced George as the drummer, and Pete Stoner replaced Larry on bass guitar. The group continued on with Dave Osborn (singer/trumpet) taking over as lead singer, Pete (bass guitar), and Phil (drums).

This is the lineup that I remember the most and got to know the best, as we (The Monzzas) rotated a lot with them on weekends and weeknights. Pete Stoner left in the spring of 1965, with Kent Fox taking his place on bass.

Chapter Three

Action Unlimited – The Beginning

In the spring of 1965, Pete Stoner left the Maroons, and they recruited Kent Fox (the Monzzas' bass player) to take his place. Kent took the job, leaving C.B. and me as the only two original members of the Monzzas. The Maroons had another change coming up shortly after that with Bill Rauth, Tom Colgan and Phil Slusher leaving the group. Chuk Trisko replaced Bill on lead guitar, Sam McIntosh replaced Tom on keyboards, and Jerry Morse replaced Phil on drums. Jerry Morse recalled his audition:

"Chuk was going to Lexington Catholic High School and had talked them into letting the band use their gym to audition new band members. I remember the gym having a stage at one end, and that's what was used for the audition. They hired me on the spot that night."

Jerry was hired, completing the lineup that would eventually become Action Unlimited— Dave, Jon, Kent, Sam, Chuk and Jerry.

Jerry Morse also recalled:

"We worked up some songs during the next few days and also put together a band uniform that consisted of matching short sleeve shirts with ascot-type Dickies that went around the neck."

The group, still called the Maroons, continued on doing private parties, playing Speck's and also landing the job of being the opening band for the Dick Clark Caravan of Stars, at EKU's Alumni Coliseum, in the spring of 1965. Kent got me a backstage pass and I watched The Maroons and all the name acts from backstage. Some of the acts on that caravan were Herman's Hermits, Little Anthony and the Imperials, Bobby Vee, Brian Hyland, plus many more.

During the show as I was standing backstage, I noticed someone came up beside me. I looked around and it was Dick Clark himself. He looked at me and smiled then left. I was in shock! Here was the guy that I watched on afternoon television all the way back in the '50s standing right beside me, a moment in life that I'll never forget.

After the show, we followed the caravan back to Richmond's Jerry's Drive In and were able to see all the acts again. I remember Little Anthony was especially giving Peter "Herman" Noone of Herman's Hermits a hard time, in a good way, on the way into the restaurant. Jerry's closed the restaurant to the public so the stars could eat in private.

Action Unlimited performing for the Dick Clark Caravan of Stars, held at Eastern Kentucky University Alumni Coliseum, Richmond, Kentucky, spring 1965

Jon recalled getting to know Herman's Hermits even better.

"My brother, Buddy Anderson, happened to be a school reporter for EKU assigned to cover the event. He spent the afternoon before the concert with the Hermits, even taking them to Speck's, Richmond's popular college bar, for lunch. He learned that the next tour stop was in our hometown of Ashland, KY and prearranged a free afternoon away for lunch at our parents' home. My mother prepared what could only be described as a Thanksgiving dinner with all the fixin's. Knowing they were British, she served tea, but with ice. Buddy and I found out later when they returned to England that a reporter interviewed them about the trip, asking what memories they brought back. Peter Noone quipped they had a tremendous meal at a lady's home in Kentucky, but she ruined the tea by putting ice in it."

Jon also remembered, during the summer of 1965, the band traveling up to Cincinnati to participate in a battle of the bands: "First prize was an appearance on the television show *Shindig!* Not having any original music, we placed second to a band that did originals named Tony and the Bandits. It was a little difficult to go on national television and do Sam and Dave unless you were Sam and Dave. The one good thing that came out of the experience was the classic 'somebody saw us.' That somebody was the assistant midwest representative of the Dick Clark Caravan of Stars. In the early '60s, the Caravan was *the* rock 'n' roll place to be. This was mega big."

The band spent a good part of the summer of '65 playing throughout Ohio, Indiana, and Wisconsin and around the Cincinnati area. Two big highlights for the band in Cincinnati were opening for The Beach Boys and backing up Billy Joe Royal.

Chuk Trisko recalled from that summer:

"We opened for the Beach Boys in Cincinnati and backstage I spoke with Dennis Wilson for a bit. He had a bandage on his head from being conked the night before from a sign thrown on stage. Brian Wilson was not touring with them at that point. After they came off the stage, they went immediately into two limos backstage and were out of there way before any audience members got backstage."

Jerry Morse also recalled another event from that night:

"I used a gold-sparkled Ludwig kit that didn't have a floor tom. I borrowed a floor tom from Phil Slusher, the former drummer for The

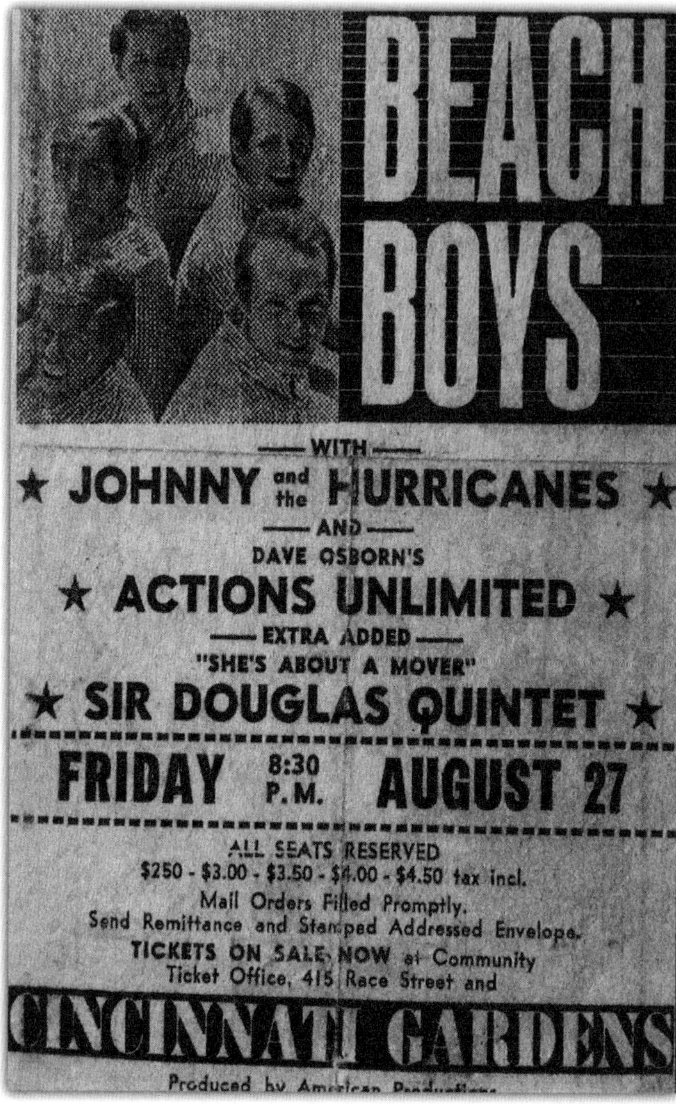

Maroons, and used it on the Beach Boys show. After the show, as we were breaking down, I realized it was gone. Someone, somehow, stole the floor tom that night before I knew it."

Chuk continued on the summer gigs:

"The Wisconsin show was in Sturgeon's Bay, across from Green Bay. As we were preparing to leave, Dave was driving his black 1949 Chevy and had just come back from his girlfriend's house in Gravel Switch, Kentucky. He had killed a rattlesnake in Gravel Switch and had

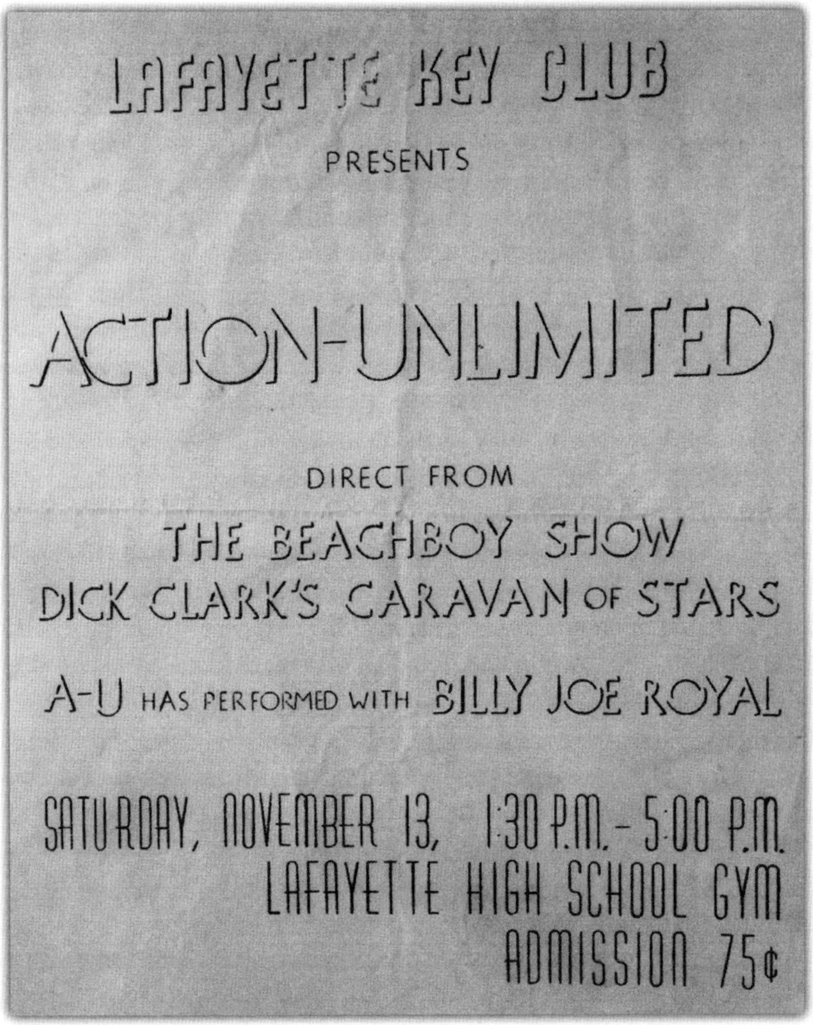

it coiled up under a shop cloth in his trunk. We were at my folks' house packing for the trip, when Jon asked Dave if he knew where something was. I don't recall what he was looking for, but Dave told him to look under the shop cloth in his trunk. When Jon pulled that cloth back, he screamed and ran up Lansdowne Drive for quite some distance, as we all laughed ourselves silly."

The band also spent time playing in Ashland, Kentucky, at The Moonlight Gardens, a very popular spot in that area. The guys stayed at Jon Anderson's home when they played in Ashland. Kent always told me about the great breakfasts that Jon's mom would fix for them every morning.

The afore-mentioned Midwest assistant for Dick Clark was Riley Kincaid, who was based in Cincinnati and worked for Peggy Rogers, who was the Midwest Representative. Riley had big plans for the band, including a possible audition in California to be the host band for the Dick Clark afternoon show *Where the Action Is*. Sometime after this, the band changed its name from The Maroons to Action Unlimited. Through the connection to Riley and Peggy, the band came back to Lexington, Kentucky to appear as the opening band on Dick Clark's Caravan of Stars. That Caravan featured Tom Jones, Peter and Gordon, The Turtles and several other national acts.

Chuk Trisko remembers the Lexington Caravan:

"I was back in the dressing room with Tom Jones. Security took him out through the crowd and came back for me. I told them I was nobody and didn't need an escort. We had to leave for Cincinnati right after the show and my change of clothes was in our gold panel truck. Security said they just wanted to clear the area, so out we went. I walked out still wearing the outfit from onstage and kids started pulling for souvenir pieces of my clothes. That and later in Trinidad, Colorado, were my two mob experiences. That was my first experience with a crowd of that size. That's when I changed the spelling of 'Chuck' to 'Chuk' because signing autographs afterwards was easier. When I got back to Lexington, the night before school started, intentionally I didn't have time to get a haircut. I walked through school in my high heel boots, hamlet-sleeved shirt and hair below my collar … the light came on … they'd all been at the concert, but had no idea it was me they had seen. When school had let out at the end of my junior year, I was a nerd with short hair, glasses, cuffed pants, etc. Suddenly, the cheerleaders, basketball players, all the 'cool' kids wanted to know me. That was a moving experience."

Kent and I were still best friends, and I remember the local newspaper (*The Winchester Sun*) doing a story on its hometown son playing on the Dick Clark Caravan of Stars. I was very proud of him. He kept me posted on all the places they were playing, and I always went to see the band whenever possible.

It was also during the time in Cincinnati that the band met a female duo named The Results, who also played at Speck's occasionally and worked with Action Unlimited on several of the Ohio, Indiana and Kentucky gigs. The Results consisted of Cincinnati natives Vicki Jones and her sister, Marti Jones. The band became close to the girls and their family as well—parents Frank and Ruth Jones, grandmother Belle, and their brother "Chip" Jones. The Jones family pretty much adopted all the guys and even let them stay at their home when they performed in the Cincinnati area. The Results had a national record release and had traveled on the road with Paul Revere and The Raiders, The Byrds and Tommy Roe, as well as several other name acts. The "A" side of their record was titled "Funky" and was written by Tommy Roe.

The band was always in close contact with Riley and Peggy throughout the summer, with them still having plans for the band to go to a higher level in the Dick Clark Organization.

Jon remembered Peggy Rogers contacting the band in the fall of 1965 and asking if the band was interested in going to California to take a shot at the big time. "She made it clear that she could guarantee nothing, and we had nothing, so it seemed like a good fit. In the ensuing months, we raised every dime we could and socked it away for The Maroons' big adventure.

In the early fall of 1965, Action Unlimited returned to Richmond, Kentucky, again playing private parties, events and Speck's. Kent called me and asked if I could sit in with the band every Thursday night at Speck's because their drummer, Jerry Morse, was going to Transylvania College in Lexington and needed Thursday nights to study. By that time, I had left The Monzzas and was not working with anyone full time. I accepted and spent the early and mid-fall sitting in with them at Speck's.

In the process, I learned all their songs and arrangements and by November felt comfortable in the drummer position. The California trip was brought up on a regular basis, but I didn't pay much attention to it, as I was only the sit-in drummer, with Jerry still being there full time. Jerry and I became good friends, and I always admired his drumming. He was a very solid drummer and had one of the best press, or buzz, rolls that I had ever heard.

When the California trip became more of a reality, I was told that Jerry might not be going because he didn't want to leave school and was asked if I would be interested in taking over his position full time and going to California with the band. Of course I said yes because I was not in school at the time and had no commitments to keep me from going.

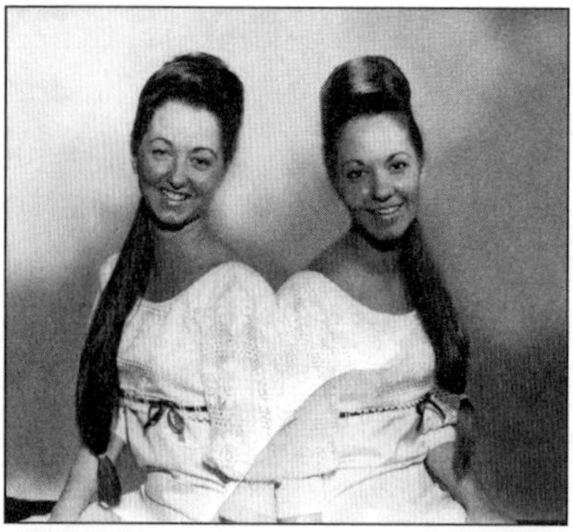

The Results—Marti and Vicki Jones—1965

Vicki and Marti Jones—The Results—rehearse with Sam McIntosh before a show in Cincinnati, 1965.

I remember one Thursday night in November after the Speck's gig Dave asked me to come by his apartment to talk. I really didn't know for sure what he wanted to talk about but had a slight suspicion it might be about joining the band full time. Kent was with me, as we always rode together to and from Speck's on the Thursday night sit-ins. When we got to the apartment, Dave, his wife Jeanne, Sam and John were gathered around the kitchen table with serious looks on their faces.

I immediately thought, "Oh no, this doesn't look good," but then Dave looked up and said, "Hey, kid, do you want to go to California? Jerry is leaving the band and we want you to go with us." I felt bad for Jerry for all the months he spent laying the groundwork for the California trip. I accepted the offer and was excited to be going, especially with Kent, as we had started out together just a couple of years earlier.

From the first band in 1963, to The Monzzas, to Action Unlimited, it was only a little over two years between when I started playing music and when I was on my way to California. It was the beginning of a great adventure.

Chapter Four

Prepping to go to California – Winter 1965

From the time I joined the band full time in November through February 1966, we played several gigs in the central Kentucky area, saving all we could from each gig to help us on the trip out to California.

I remember one eventful weekend during December of '65 at the Club 68 in Lebanon, Kentucky. The weather was good when we left, but by the time we arrived, we ran into a raging snowstorm. We played the gig and came out to see a winter wonderland of snow and ice. Dave's wife, Jeanne, was from Gravel Switch, Kentucky, which was not too far from Lebanon, and we all knew we couldn't drive back that night as all the roads were really in bad shape. She told us we could stay at an empty farmhouse in Gravel Switch that belonged to her family, if we could make it there.

Somehow we made it and set up camp in the house, which did have a pot-bellied stove that didn't put out much heat and spent the next two nights there until the roads cleared enough for us to get back home on the following Monday. The house did have electricity, and Jeanne supplied us with enough electric blankets to sleep under that kept us warm during those nights. The next morning we were close enough to walk in the snow down to Penn's Grocery for breakfast and sit in front of a huge wood stove to keep warm. Needless to say, we spent a lot of time during those two days in front of that stove.

Later that month, we played a high school Christmas dance in Winchester, Kentucky, for George Rogers Clark High School, and the audience was quite taken with our band outfits. During the summer of '65, the band had bought dress jackets with a tiger skin design and knee-high black boots. We wore the jackets with black turtleneck pullovers and black pants. It was a very unique band uniform. I was the only one without the black boots, as it was hard for me to play the drums with the boots on.

Chuk Trisko on the band uniforms:

"We were looking for uniforms and went into a clothing store in downtown Lexington. We saw the tiger skin coats and knew that was it. Black pants, turtlenecks and boots were all that would work with them because they were so bold."

In December, we had a meeting with Peggy Rogers and Riley Kincaid at Kent's apartment in Lexington to talk about and plan our upcoming trip to the West Coast. Peggy explained that Riley would become our manager on the West Coast, and that she would go out first and have everything ready for us when we got there. They laid out the pros and cons of what we could expect and again, as Jon Anderson mentioned before, promising nothing for sure on the possible audition for the Dick Clark show but giving us hope that we would have a good shot at it.

I remember sitting on the couch when Peggy walked over to me, cupped my chin in her hand, and said, "You're going to look good on camera." I think we thought, at that time, that we had the job but little did we know that things could change so quickly in the music business. We even set a target date to leave in early February of 1966. There was talk that we would go to Atlanta first and work with Tommy Roe, but that changed a few weeks later to us going straight on out to California. It was also decided that Vicki and Marti Jones of The Results would go out with us as a package deal, especially with them having already had a national record release. Riley felt it would be good for both us and them to work together.

We worked a couple of gigs in January 1966 but spent a lot of time saving, planning and prepping for the trip. The word had gotten out that Action Unlimited was going to California to audition for a major television show, and there was a lot of support and excitement from our friends, families and fans, especially in the central Kentucky area.

The last gig we played before we left in early February was at a fraternity party at Centre College in Danville, Kentucky. Ironically, Gary Edwards and The Embers were playing at a frat house next door, and we went over on our breaks to hear them. Gary's drummer was none other than Bud Ecton, who was my early mentor and one of the finest drummers around. I again stood to the side, as I did when I was just starting out, and watched every move he made on the kit. I was absolutely astounded at how good he was. I didn't get to talk to Bud that night, but I hoped that he would be proud of what I had accomplished in such a short time.

We finished the gig, packed up and headed out, stopping at a restaurant on Danville's main street to fill our bellies for the long drive to California. We were finally on our way.

Chapter Five

The Adventure Begins – February 1966

Action Unlimited was composed of six musicians from all parts of the state of Kentucky. Dave Osborn was from Louisville, Jon Anderson from Ashland, Sam McIntosh from Jackson, Chuk Trisko from Lexington, and Kent Fox and me from Winchester. Before you join us on our journey, it might be good to review the lives of the people you're traveling with:

Dave Osborn

Dave Osborn was the lead singer and trumpet player for AU. Dave was the oldest member and the leader of the group. He was our rock, our father figure, the one we went to with any problems. He was very levelheaded, a visionary, always seemed to know the right path to take. Dave had been with The Maroons since their early beginnings and was a music major at EKU. He was a really good showman on stage and, being from Louisville, had been exposed to all the Louisville groups that were so predominant throughout Kentucky, therefore knowing what kind of standard to set for Action Unlimited. The previous years that he had spent with The Maroons, Gary Edwards and all the other talented musicians in that group gave him the experience and ability to lead in a special way. Dave was married to Jeanne Lane, who was from Gravel Switch and part of the family that owned the well-known Penn's Country Store. Jeanne became pregnant and had twins, Dava and Dawn, in December 1965. I remember all of us in the band going to the hospital to see her and the girls after they were born. After our visit, when we were in the parking lot, Jean came to the window, holding the twins up for us to see. I know Dave was proud that night as I remember looking at him and seeing the tears in his eyes. Dave was 23 years old when the group left for California.

Jon Anderson

Jon Anderson was a singer and the saxophone player for AU. Jon was a student at EKU and one of the early members of The Maroons. He started playing the saxophone during grade school, continued with it through high school, eventually playing sax in The Maroons during his college years. Jon was the ultimate showman of the group and the co-leader with Dave Osborn, as they were the two oldest members of the group. Jon was also the comedian on stage and did most of the choreography of the floor shows staged by the group. His father owned a drugstore in Ashland, and his family opened their home to the group when they performed in the Ashland area. Jon was well known throughout the EKU campus, easygoing and fun to be around. Jon was 23 years old when the group left for California.

Sam McIntosh

Sam McIntosh was a singer and the keyboard player for AU and was also a student at EKU. He began playing keyboards during high school with several groups around the Jackson and Hazard, Kentucky areas. Sam joined Action Unlimited in the spring of 1965, taking over Tom Colgan's place. Sam was the soul singer in the group, as he had the right kind of voice for that style. Sam was probably the tallest member, being over six foot. He was also well known on campus with his outgoing personality and love for mischievous pranks. Sam was 21 when the group left for California.

Chuk Trisko was the lead guitar player for AU and the youngest member of the group. AU hired Chuk when he was a junior in high school in the spring of 1965. He often recalled that he was hired by the band because he showed up for the audition and several shows

Chuk Trisko

afterwards and was the only one who showed enough interest by watching them play for entire shows, hours at a time. Chuk started out playing drums, changed to guitar, and had only been playing for a year when he was hired as AU's lead guitar player. He was a complete natural, not only on guitar but also as a songwriter, writing the songs later for AU's first record. Chuk was 18 when the group left for California.

Kent Fox

Kent Fox was a singer and the bass player for AU. Kent started taking piano lessons at age seven and continued on through grade and high school in music. He also played the saxophone in the high school marching band. Kent attended EKU during the fall of 1965. He played guitar in his first band, The Big B's, along with C.B. Spicer, who was also in that band. Kent was one of the founding members of the Monzzas, with C.B. and me, starting first as their guitar player and then eventually moving to the bass guitar. Kent joined The Maroons in the spring of 1965 as their bass player and was there when the name was changed to Action Unlimited. Kent was tall, blond and one of the most popular with the Action Unlimited audiences. Kent was 18 when the group left for California.

Dewey Pope

I, ***Dewey Pope***, was the drummer for AU. I joined Action Unlimited in the late fall of 1965, taking over the drumming duties from Jerry Morse. I started my drumming career in 1962, soaking up everything I could from watching other drummers and finally taking lessons from Cecil Jones, a drum teacher in Lexington. I graduated from George Rogers Clark High School in June 1964 and attended college the following fall but eventually left to concentrate on my music. I co-founded The Monzzas, along with Kent Fox and C.B. Spicer, in 1963. I, along with Sam, enjoyed being a prankster in AU, always doing something to get a reaction out of the rest of the guys. I was 19 when the group left for California.

After the gig at Centre College, we packed up and hit the road. Our original plan was to take Route 66 all the way out. We headed out of Kentucky and up through Illinois to pick up 66. Now, you have to picture our transportation. A very popular thing for music groups in the '60s was to purchase used funeral home hearses and convert them to band vehicles. AU had done that. The band had a 1953 Cadillac hearse, which of course was black, and had Action Unlimited painted on the sides in gold, which made sense since AU is the chemical element symbol for gold. AU also had a 1956 Ford panel truck that replaced the original red GMC panel truck that The Maroons used. Kent's uncle, Neville Cotton, who had a farm just outside Richmond, let the band use his garage and barn to work on the truck. Kent recalls:

"The panel truck needed work, so Sam rebuilt the engine in my Uncle Neville's garage. There was a barn just across from the garage, and that's where the truck was painted. Sam was a good mechanic, and that saved us a lot of money."

The band painted the truck gold themselves, as former drummer Jerry Morse recalled:

"I remember that panel truck and helping to paint it gold. Kent's uncle let us use his barn, and some of us got together and painted the entire truck with hand brushes."

Jeanne (Lane) Osborn (Dave's wife) recalled that she had wanted to paint the name Action Unlimited on the sides because she was an art major at Eastern, but the job went to Sam instead because of his previous experience as a sign painter. Sam had a lot of talents, including being a mechanic, artist and musician.

The panel truck was used mainly for band equipment, and by the time we got Sam's Hammond B3, Leslie, my drums and all the other equipment in, we didn't have much room left. I remember it having lots of play in the steering wheel, so it was a real challenge keeping it on the road. But both were in good running order, at least when we left, and packed to the gills with equipment and personal items. We did leave enough room in the back of the hearse for us to sleep while others were driving, as we planned to drive straight through.

1953 Cadillac hearse and 1956 Ford Panel Truck with Chuk, Dave, Jon, Dewey and Sam

As we were driving through Illinois, the hearse broke down in a small town (name unknown) and would not go any farther. Luckily, we found a garage that opened up for us on a Sunday afternoon and started to work early the next morning on fixing it. We spent the night in the hearse and truck, finding whatever room we could to sleep. It was tough, but we managed. The people in that small town got lots of laughs seeing a funeral hearse with Action Unlimited painted on the sides. We actually got lots of stares all the way from Kentucky to California from that sight. (Later, in California, we added a 1953 black Cadillac sedan to the fleet).

By mid-day on Monday we were on our way again and back in good spirits. We picked up Route 66 and were in awe of the fact that we were actually traveling on the highway made famous by the television show a few years earlier. I slept a lot, especially when I wasn't at my turn driving, so I missed a lot of the sights but do remember waking up early one morning in the back of the hearse, looking out the window and seeing mountains in the distance and huge boulders right beside the road. I asked one of the guys where we were, and they said New Mexico. When we arrived in Albuquerque, we decided to stop and eat. We saw several taco stands and being from Kentucky, which didn't have many Mexican restaurants or stands, we decided to try one. It was a good choice, as the tacos were delicious.

After eating, we headed out again, and I remember it was sunny but cold and windy. I was driving the hearse, and right outside the city we started up a long hill. Just as we topped the hill, we ran into a blinding snowstorm. The road suddenly turned to ice, and the hearse decided to do a 360-degree turn with us stopping on the other side on the shoulder. Thankfully, no other vehicles were coming toward us on that side of the road. Chuck and Dave were asleep in the back of the hearse, waking up quickly due to the violent turning and shifting of the vehicle, with looks of fear on their faces. Kent was riding in the front seat of the hearse with me and also had a look of fear on his face. After we came to a stop, I quietly opened the door of the hearse, got out and walked over to the panel truck, which was behind us and had stopped on the other side of the road. As I opened the door of the truck, I noticed that Jon and Sam were in shock as well. We always carried a fifth of Kentucky bourbon behind the front seat of the truck, so I reached behind the seat, took the cap off and had a long swig of straight whiskey. It brought me back to life as I was in more shock than anyone else. I looked up at Jon and Sam and said, "Someone else can drive the hearse. That's it for me, at least for now." After that, we all broke out into laughter, thanking God at the same time. I did take that break from driving but before long was back at the wheel and heading toward California.

After the ice rink escapade in New Mexico, we traveled on through Arizona, suffering another vehicle breakdown but nothing major, and crossed over into California at Needles with good weather. From there we traveled on down into southern California, eventually reaching our destination, Los Angeles. So, in looking back, we had picked up Route 66 in Illinois, taking us through Missouri, Kansas, Oklahoma, Texas, New Mexico, Arizona, and finally into California. We had broken down in Illinois, had a fight with a snowstorm in New Mexico and a minor breakdown in Arizona, but we made it. It was February 1966, and we were in California.

Chapter Six

California

From the California border on into Los Angeles, I was mesmerized at the difference in the landscape from what we were used to in Kentucky. I remember going through several communities on the way to LA, and it almost seemed like another planet, as it was so different. When we reached the outskirts of Los Angeles, it then became an endless landscape of houses, buildings and tall palm trees. We continued on to the address given to us by Riley Kincaid, which turned out to be, of all places, in Hollywood.

Riley, Vicki, Marti, Jon's brother Buddy and a couple of others had already come out before and were waiting for us. The apartment where we were meeting belonged to Riley's ex-husband Russ Kincaid. We pulled into the apartment complex on Wednesday night, piled out of the vehicles, and almost kissed the ground as a testament to the fact that we had made it all the way from Kentucky. Riley came out to meet us, along with the others, and we had a brief reunion before heading inside.

When we got inside and settled down in the living room with food and refreshments, Riley came out and said these words: "Well, guys, I've got good news and bad news; which do you want first?" Dave then replied with, "Give us the bad news first," upon which she told us that the audition for *Where the Action Is* was off as another band had gotten the job. So, here we were, traveling all the way from Kentucky, some 3,000 miles, for a dream-come-true audition, and it was not going to happen. I remember there was an eerie silence, especially from all the band members, in the room and a sense of "What are we going to do now? Go back home? After all the fanfare of leaving Kentucky for this opportunity and having it disappear in front of us?" But we also had to remember that Peggy and Riley both had warned us before we left

Kentucky that no guarantees could be made, and that had come true. Kent and I especially looked at each other with a look of disappointment on our faces, thinking, "How would we explain this to our family and friends back in Winchester?"

Riley then continued on with, "But all is not lost. The good news is that I have you an audition at The Trip club on Sunset Strip for a two-week engagement at The Red Velvet club, which is one of the hottest clubs on the Sunset Strip." Riley also went on to explain that she had left Dick Clark as a regional representative but was still affiliated with the organization. She was going to take over total management of our group and promised us that she could make great things happen. We had an impromptu band meeting there in the living room and decided in a unanimous vote that we were going to stay, do the audition for the Red Velvet and take our chances on Riley's promise. So, things had changed drastically in just a few minutes in that apartment living room, but we were there and we knew in our hearts that we could make it work. We knew that we had a great band, and it was also at that point that we decided that we were going to make it—that whatever it took, we were going to make this a worthwhile venture.

According to Jon Anderson, "Now, our new manager had a propensity for gin. After a half dozen gin and what-evers, her eyes would roll back in her head, but she never broke stride with her conversation. When they rolled, you never know if she was speaking to you or the ceiling. I only mention this because it points to the fact that, as long as she had a pulse, she was promoting the band. She cornered a booking agent in Hollywood the first week we were there, and we were off and running on the club circuit. We developed a solid club circuit from Palm Springs, California in the south to Portland, Oregon in the north and Las Vegas, Nevada to the east. This built our credibility and gave our manager ample flexibility scheduling the right people to catch us. Things looked promising."

The audition at the Trip took place on Friday night of that first week after arriving on Wednesday night. We didn't have much time to prepare, but we felt confident that we would do fine. The Trip was one of the most popular clubs on the Strip and had been featured in both movies and television. We were somewhat star-struck just being in the building, but we had to put that aside and perform. We did the audition and before we got out of the building were told that we would be starting at the Red Velvet on the following Monday night. We had no idea what lay ahead of us, but Riley had come through on her first promise of great things to happen.

I remember loading in at the Red Velvet on the first day. It was a club with a large dance floor, large stage on the back wall, with the outer three walls having booths that were a step or two up from the floor level. The front wall, to the left of the entrance, had a long club-length bar. I also remember the outside entrance having a red canopy with the name Red Velvet on it.

One of the first things we did, on Saturday of that first weekend, was to shop in Hollywood for some hip clothes, as we felt we needed to look more like a rock band, especially in Hollywood. We found a store in Hollywood, and all of us purchased bell-bottom pants and hamlet-style shirts, which were a far cry from what we had worn in Kentucky.

From the very first night, we started seeing celebrities come into the club, leading to us being even more star-struck than we were at The Trip club, just down the street. Another big difference from the clubs in Kentucky was that we played from 9 p.m. till 2 a.m., five full sets. That was a long time, but we didn't care, as the nights always seemed to fly by. I remember Paul Peterson from *The Donna Reed Show* coming in quite often during our time there. We got to meet him, as well as Richard Davis, one of Elvis Presley's bodyguards, who took a great liking to the band because of the Kentucky/Tennessee connection. Richard came in just about every night and was very friendly and complimentary of the band. We met Donna O'Connor, who was the daughter of the famous actor Donald O'Connor. I also remember one night playing on stage and looking out to my right, up into the booth area, and seeing the group The Knickerbockers, who had the hit record "Lies" at that time. We got to meet them as well. They were a great group of guys.

Jimmy Walker, the drummer for The Knickerbockers, recalled the following about The Red Velvet in an interview with Gary James for his webpage classicbands.com:

"The Red Velvet … on Sunset Boulevard. It was sort of a watering hole for people that didn't want to be bothered, you know, famous rock stars would come in there where they could have a few drinks and tourists didn't know anything about it. So, it was an offbeat kind of place. … (It) was where the people on the *Shindig* show would come and hang out. If you went down the Strip and you went to The Whisky a Go-Go or The Trip … you'd get besieged by fans. This place, nobody knew about it. The whole Beach Boy crew came … The Four Seasons used to come in. Chicago came in. That's where I met The Righteous Brothers … The Lovin' Spoonful used to come in … The guys from Buffalo Springfield came in all the time. It was that kind of place. At the time, it was a real exciting time in the music business. In L.A. there were a lot of TV shows that were being done on music … there was Dick Clark's *Where The Action Is*, which we became regulars on later."

One night Roy Head was in the club, and he came up and sat in with us, doing his major hit record "Treat Her Right." Chuk Trisko, our lead guitar player, had his guitar stolen from the upstairs office of the club, and Riley, through her connections, borrowed a guitar from the guitarist of Sam the Sham and the Pharaohs until Chuk could get another one.

Tuesday nights were the open mike or jam nights and we had several celebrity musicians who would come up and sit in, including The Coasters the second week. One night there was a buzz going around the club that Johnny Rivers was in the room. When we took our break, I made it a point to try to find him. I did finally see him standing back by the bar with a multitude of people around him. I didn't get to meet him but at least got to see him from a distance.

We lived at Russ Kincaid's apartment during the two-week period we were at the club and it got pretty crowded at times, but we endured. We had a great reception from the club crowds every night, and of course, that boosted our morale to the point that someone in the band mentioned that we were "the hit of the town." But little did we know that we were just another band among many that congregated in Los Angeles to fulfill their dreams.

Also, we took time to explore Hollywood, going to the Cinerama Theater on the Strip to see the movie *Battle of the Bulge*, visiting Grauman's Chinese Theatre to see all the famous hand and footprints in the sidewalk, taking a drive to Malibu's famous beach/residential area and, finally, visiting Beverly Hills to see all the movie star homes. On our night off, Kent and I decided to take a walk down the Strip to see the sights. As we walked along, we saw a group of people coming toward us, and one person stood out who looked very familiar. When they passed us, I looked over, and it was Leslie Nielson, who was a major television star at the time and went on to become even more famous from the *Airplane* and *Naked Gun* movies. The Red Velvet was truly our indoctrination to the wonders of Hollywood, which was still magic at that time.

Another eventful happening during the two-week stint was the Paramount Studio Tour. One of the people who we met at Russ's apartment complex was a security guard at Paramount Studios, which was very close to us. He was from Ohio, and naturally we got to be good friends with him. He mentioned that he could give us a personal guided tour of the studios, and we gladly accepted. We picked a day, arriving early in the morning at the front gate, where he met us and then he took us in for one of the most fantastic events of my life.

We toured all the main buildings, having access that most of the tourists didn't because of his connections as a security guard. One of the main attractions we saw was the set of the popular Western *Bonanza*. We actually got to watch Michael Landon film a scene on the streets of the town, Virginia City. We also were able to visit all the interior sets, seeing the town saloon and the bedrooms and living room of the Ponderosa ranch house. Now, this is a Western that I had been watching on television for several years, and here I was, right in the middle of it. One of the most amazing sights was that the ranch house was inside a huge building. We were told that the riders on horseback always had to enter from the left side of the barn, as they had to start in from the street outside. On the way from one building to another, we went by a trailer that turned out to be Lorne Greene's. He came to the door just as we walked by and smiled at us.

On the outside set of Virginia City, there was a huge painted landscape of mountains and sky, and we were told that it was used in the movie *The Ten Commandants*. We also were taken by Elvis Presley and Ann Margaret's dressing rooms and saw several other sets used in countless movies. This was magic, and we all loved it—another part of our indoctrination to Hollywood.

Also during that time, Riley got us into the Vince Demattia Public Relations group, and they set up a publicity shoot at Griffith Park. Griffith Park was a major landmark in Hollywood, located on Mount Hollywood. You can also see the Hollywood sign from the park. There is an observatory on the summit, and after the photo shoot, we visited it and learned that several major movies and television shows had been filmed there, including the classic *Rebel Without A Cause* with James Dean. The photographer located a huge boulder on the grounds and decided to pose the band on and around it. We all were wearing our newly purchased bell-bottoms and hamlet shirts and felt like we were truly rock stars. The photo was well done and is still treasured by all the members of the group. The picture shown on page 102 has our autographs on it, as this was one that was sent back home to Kentucky for our families and friends.

Chapter Seven

Thunderbird Hotel - Las Vegas

During the second week of our stint at The Red Velvet, Riley broke the news to us that our next gig would be in Las Vegas at the Thunderbird Hotel. Again, Riley was coming through with her promise of doing great things for us. We finished up at the Velvet on Saturday night, packed up the vehicles, and headed out for Las Vegas.

The two-week period in Hollywood had been almost like a dream, especially playing on one of the most famous strips in America, and now we were on our way to play on another famous strip. The Strip in Las Vegas was about as famous as you can get, and we were playing there in just a very short time after arriving in California. I remember seeing Las Vegas in movies and on television but didn't have any idea of what it would actually be like in person. In the mid-'60s, there was the Strip and downtown. There was still some separation from the two in those days, but they were still connected by business and residential areas.

We arrived and found our motel on the Strip, which seemed to be located right in the middle of several wedding chapels, and unloaded our personal items. As we headed to the Thunderbird, we then saw all the famous hotel/casinos I had heard about over the years—the Flamingo, the Sands, the Dunes, the Sahara and finally, the Thunderbird.

The fourth resort to open on the Las Vegas Strip, the Thunderbird Hotel featured Native-American themed décor and a Navajo-themed restaurant. Of course, the hotel had a showroom, but unlike any other place on the Strip, the Thunderbird had a bowling alley.

We arrived during daylight hours, so we hadn't experienced the sight of all the lights that make Vegas a wonderland of neon during the dark hours. The front entrance of the Thunderbird was very impressive, with cars pulling up and people everywhere. We went in and found out where we were supposed to load in, and again, you can imagine the stares we got when a Cadillac hearse and gold panel truck with Action Unlimited painted on the sides pulled up to the front door.

After we were rerouted to the rear of the hotel, we went in and found our way to the stage area and started unloading. To the front of the stage was a tiered area of booths and tables. The entire room, stage and audience area, was huge, and even as were setting up our equipment there were people in the booths and tables, eating and drinking. We also had to set the drums, keyboards and amps up on wheeled platforms so they could be wheeled back and forth on and off the stage as there were several other shows going on besides us.

Riley arrived and informed us that we would have an afternoon rehearsal with the dancers. Dancers? We didn't know about any dancers, but it was Vegas, and we just figured it was the norm. We had just enough time to get everything set up when the dancers arrived. Riley introduced us to the ladies, and they were beautiful, professional and very nice to us.

We went through our sets, picked out the songs they would be dancing on, and rehearsed, after which Riley called a meeting with the band. She then told us that we were the rock 'n' roll show that would go on at 4 a.m., play for an hour, take a half hour break, go back on at 5:30 a.m. and play another hour—two one-hour sets. I remember Sam and Chuk looking puzzled at Riley and saying, "Why are we going on at that early hour in the morning? Everybody will be home asleep!" Neither they, nor any of the rest of us in the band, had figured out that Las Vegas was a 24-hour marathon—nobody slept. Vegas literally was a 24/7 environment, one big party.

Also, the other plus was that we were making big money for this two-week engagement. We did quite well at The Red Velvet, but this was even more. I was starting to think that Riley Kincaid was a miracle worker to bring an unknown band from Kentucky into these best-known clubs and get us the kind of pay we were getting. Again, she was coming through on her promises.

We finished the rehearsal and band meeting and headed back to the motel to grab some rest and get ready for our opening show, which was that night, or should I say, morning. We all paired up, two to a room at the motel, which worked out to be Kent and me, Jon and Dave, and Chuk and Sam. Every room had a balcony, and it was fun to walk out and watch the non-stop traffic and people everywhere you looked. It seemed like forever waiting to go back to the Thunderbird in the early morning hours, and most of all it was really messing with our bodies' time clocks. We did decide to get there early enough so we could see some of the other acts on before us. They were all great, capturing our attention so much that 4 a.m. came around pretty quickly.

I remember watching the platforms roll out with our equipment, climbing up behind the drums, looking over and seeing Sam on his platform with Dave, Jon, Kent and Chuk out in front of us, and finally it was time. We got the cue from the stage manager, the emcee came out and introduced us, the curtain opened, and I immediately started into the drum groove for "Land of a Thousand Dances."

I knew the dancers would be coming out on the first number, but I was not prepared, nor were any of the rest of us, for what happened next. They came out from both sides of the stage, working their way around to the front and middle of the stage, and as I looked around I saw that they were topless. Now Riley didn't tell us about this. She later said it was to be a surprise, and believe me, it was. We should have known, but again, we were a young Kentucky band playing for the first time in Las Vegas and had no idea this was part of the show. After our shock and awe on the first number that first night, we got used to it for the next two weeks. After all, this was Las Vegas and we were professionals, whether we knew it or not.

It was really strange after finishing the second show and walking out to the bright morning daylight to go back to the motel. We were used to coming out in the darkness of late night hours after a gig, but this was early morning. It was hard getting used to.

It was in Las Vegas that Dave gave me some of the best advice that I had ever been given as a musician. I was young, fearless and wanted to be impressive but was guilty of overplaying at times. We were waiting to go on one night and Dave and I were standing backstage, talking music. I respected his opinion and knowledge of music very much and was asking him about dynamics and music performance in general. He was a music major and a tremendous mentor, especially with me only having three years of experience under my belt. He explained: "First, don't show everything you know in the first song" and "second, think dynamics. Know when to take a song up and when to bring it back down." What he was telling me, in a mentoring way, was to be conscious of overplaying and dynamic effects (when to change from the hi-hat to the ride cymbal, playing softer, louder etc.) to help the band. He was right, and from that point on, I really concentrated on being more of a team player for the group. It was great advice that I never forgot in my entire career.

Another big event for me during the Las Vegas engagement was a reunion with my older brother, Bob, whom I hadn't seen for many years. The band went into a restaurant on the second day we were there, and after sitting down at the bar, I happened to glance through the door into the kitchen and saw him. I jumped up and ran back through the kitchen door to greet him. He had spent many years studying to be a chef, and there he was in Las Vegas. My sister had told me he was there but didn't know where. We had a great reunion and spent a lot of time together the next two weeks. He took all of us in the band to Lake Mead for a tour of Hoover Dam and a boat excursion on the lake and also treated us to some great meals, as he knew all the best restaurants in the area.

One night during the second week, Kent and I were talking to the stage manager before we went on. We had gotten to know him, and he took a great liking to us and our band. He had been in Vegas all his life and knew the ropes on the Strip and downtown, as well. Of course, Kent, Chuk and I were underage, keeping somewhat of a low profile, and he figured that out pretty quickly. He told us that night that we had something to tell our grandchildren about someday. We were playing at our young ages on the Strip in Las Vegas, and that many musicians and entertainers worked hard all their lives in downtown Vegas and never made it to the Strip or, if they did, it was a long dues-paying process. We didn't realize that the Strip was considered that much more important than the downtown area. Las Vegas was a great learning experience for us all.

There was one drummer I watched every night on the show right before us. He was, of course, much older and more experienced than I was, using fills and grooves with a lot of Latin influence. He was one of the first drummers I saw that used rim shots a lot on the snare, even on his grooves. I talked to him about this, and he explained the technique to me. I was used to playing more on the top and middle of the snare. He also switched from traditional grip to the overhand grip (matched grip) a lot during his playing. I remember Ringo Starr of The Beatles using the overhand grip but had never considered using it myself. I had started out using the traditional grip and was pretty locked into that technique.

I saw many different styles of drumming, from Big Band to Latin to very impressive show drumming that was very typical in Vegas. It was an education and eye opening for me to the point that I began to consider how to improve my drumming. Riley had mentioned to me that she had a good friend in San Diego who was the percussionist for the San Diego Symphony and a teacher. I would later take advantage of this and study under him every time we were close to that area.

During the latter part of the second week, Riley told us that after finishing in Vegas, we were going back to L.A. for a couple of days and then we were leaving on a two-week tour that would take us all the way from California to Kansas, City, Missouri and back.

Chapter Eight
The Tour

Riley told us the tour was sanctioned by Dick Clark and would have the Dick Clark heading but would not be a "Caravan of Stars" type. The girls, The Results, would be one of the acts, along with us, and the headliner would be George McCannon, III, who had several records, with a hit record a couple of years earlier. We would have opening acts at all the different stops, but the main acts were the girls, George and us.

We would also not be on a bus but would be taking our own vehicles—the hearse and panel truck. I remember we were really concerned that both would make it all the way there and back. Nevertheless, we packed up again and headed out. We were going to meet George in Albuquerque, New Mexico, and then head on to Trinidad, Colorado, the first stop on the tour.

We made it to Albuquerque with no problems. Most of us stayed at the motel while Dave and Riley, who accompanied us on the tour, went to the airport to pick up George. When they arrived back at the motel, we had decided to greet George with a good old Kentucky welcome, "the Moon," thinking this would go over well and ease any first meeting tensions that might exist. When he walked in the door, the first thing he saw was the majority of us "mooning" him, and I'm sure this was quite a sight. We learned right off the bat that George was all business and was not impressed with our greeting, so we had not gotten off to a good start with him.

He did make adjustments to tolerate us that night, and we headed out toward Trinidad, Colorado the next morning. We drove all day and, by the late afternoon, ran into a severe snowstorm going over the Raton pass from New Mexico into Colorado. I was driving the panel truck, with all the play in the wheel, and it was really scary trying to stay on the icy road, especially going downhill. Riley was in the front seat with me, and we were both really scared that we were going to go off the side of mountain before we made it through the storm. I remember coming down the mountain and seeing a stoplight in the distance, knowing that I had to stop. I started feathering the brakes, trying to control the sway of the truck from the wheel play and feeling us sliding, all at the same time. Somehow, I got the truck stopped in time, but Riley and I were both nervous wrecks. I don't know what it was, but every time we hit any kind of storm it was always me driving one of the two vehicles. I don't remember who was driving the hearse but didn't hear about any problems.

We made it into Trinidad early the next morning, and if I remember correctly, it was a mining town, not very large, located at the foot of the Raton Pass along the Santa Fe Trail. We were going to be performing at the high school gymnasium, and there were posters all over town announcing the concert. We found the school, unloaded for our performance that night, and spent the day exploring the town stores. Everywhere we went, the locals treated us like celebrities, as they didn't have many rock 'n' roll tours coming to town. We went to a restaurant and ordered lunch, but they wouldn't let us pay. It was a great boost to our morale for the show coming up later that night.

Showtime finally arrived and the show started with The Results, then George McCannon and us as their backup band and final act. This lineup changed several times during the tour, but we were the last ones on that particular night. George started his segment of the show off with a cover of Roy Orbison's "Pretty Woman." He loved that song and followed it with his record hits that we pretty much winged it on, as we hadn't had any rehearsal time with him before the tour. He had sent copies to us by Riley for us to listen to and learn before he arrived. There was no problem with the girls' records, as we had worked with them before many times and knew the arrangements.

The gym was packed, especially with young teenage girls, screaming, yelling and pushing up as close to the stage as they could. Chuk Trisko recalled:

"I also remembered being mobbed while Jon did 'Please, Please, Please,' the James Brown number where we (he and Jon) got into a mock fight (part of the floor show). As I recall, it was the first rock 'n' roll show they'd ever had there, and the girls had pulled up close to the stage. I remember Jon asking me if I was going to do the fall off the stage or not. I figured I could get down to the floor and back up before they knew what happened, but when I did it, my foot got tangled in the mic cord and I was hanging from the stage. They came off their seats, and I was kissed from head to foot. I saw an arm with that tiger jacket reaching down and someone saying, 'grab hold' as Dave pulled me back onstage and the curtains closed over my legs."

After the curtain closed and we collected Chuk back onto the stage, we could still hear the girls screaming out front. Someone opened the curtain back up and they were still pushed up against the front of the stage, wanting us to come over. I went over to the edge of the stage and bent down to sign an autograph and was grabbed by both of my arms and pulled forward. At the same time, one of the security guards saw this, came running over, and grabbed me around the waist, pulling in the other direction. I literally thought I was going to be pulled apart but loved it. Kent, Dave, Sam and Jon were all fighting them off as well and I think each and every one of us truly enjoyed it. I remember Chuk running back over and doing a swan dive right into the crowd of girls. Finally, the security guard wrestled me away from the girls, and we closed the curtain a final time and did not open it again. Chuk somehow got away from the girls and showed up backstage, looking pretty messed up but with a smile on his face.

We had to pack up right after the show and get back on the road because we had a show the next night in Hastings, Nebraska. By the time we made it outside, the girls had left, and we loaded the vehicles and started toward Nebraska. Trinidad was definitely one of the highlights of the tour. In addition to Hastings, we had concerts coming up in Hays, Kansas; St. Joseph, Missouri; Kansas City, Missouri; Kansas City, Kansas; and Lawrence, Kansas. The one thing that I remember most about going to Hastings, Nebraska was the long drive from Trinidad and the tumbleweeds—they were everywhere.

The Hastings concert went well, and we again packed up after the concert and headed out for Hays, Kansas. We played at a university in Hays, Kansas, that had a student environment and a party atmosphere. Jon remembered that concert as being one of the best on the tour. We then headed for St. Joseph and had a great concert and reception there, as well.

By this time, we were worn out from the one-nighters and constant traveling. We had a short break from St. Joseph to Kansas City,

Missouri and Kansas City, Kansas. Kansas City, Kansas was eventful due to a group of angry parents. We played the concert and had a motel night's stay before heading out the next morning. This was another concert with the screaming young girls, and after we got back to the motel, we had all gathered in one room to make plans for the next leg of the tour when we heard a knock at the door. Sam opened the door to a large group of young girls wanting to come in and party with the band. I think he was strongly considering letting them in, when no sooner than he opened the door, a group of cars pulled into the parking lot with parents piling out, heading straight toward us. They immediately rounded the girls up and left. Riley came over from her room to check out the disturbance and was quite relieved when she found out the parents had collected the girls, preventing any further problems.

We left the next morning and finished up the tour in Lawrence, Kansas at the Red Dog Inn, which was a converted movie theater. We again were the last act on stage, and as we looked up toward the projection booth, high in the rear of the theater, we saw something strange out of one of the projection openings. It was George mooning us. I'm sure the audience was wondering what we were laughing so hard at, but we didn't let them know what was happening. We had become very close to him during the past two weeks and converted him from being all business at the beginning of the tour to one of the guys. George was a great guy, very talented and a pleasure to spend that two-week tour with. He left us after Lawrence, flying back, with us having a long journey back to California in the hearse and panel truck.

The girls, The Results, had really performed great, as well, and were a great asset to the tour. We learned a lot from them as they had already been out on tour and were the seasoned performers compared to us being the "newbies." Riley's plan was for them to stay in L.A. after we got back so they could work on their promotion plans.

By this time, the weather was starting to get better, so we didn't have any snowstorms to contend with and made it back to L.A. with no problems. Chuk did remember one occasion when he was driving behind Kent, who was driving the panel truck at the time:

"Kent put on his left blinker, pulled into the left lane, sped up, put on his right blinker, and pulled into the right lane again. When he saw us behind him in the hearse, he pulled over and told us he had seen another car and passed it. Trouble was, there was no other car. We switched drivers at that point."

It was a tiresome drive, but we made it. During the trip back, Riley informed us that our next engagement was at a club in Sacramento, California, but that we had a couple of days in L.A. before having to be there. We needed the rest, as the tour took a lot out of us.

Chapter Nine

Sacramento, CA - Hilton Inn - San Francisco

After a couple days' rest, we left out again for Sacramento for a two-week engagement at a club there. Sacramento is the capital city of California. I don't remember the name of the club, but do remember it was large and very popular in the area.

The first day we were there, the owner was looking at Chuk, Kent and me pretty closely, probably wondering if we were old enough to be playing in clubs. We were not 21 by any means, but I'm sure there were lots of bands on the West Coast with underage musicians. After we finished setting up, Sam and I went to the bar and asked for a drink. The bartender suggested that we try his specialty, "the Killer," upon which I said, "Sure, why not?"

I knew as I watched him mix the Killer that it was a mistake because he poured a little bit of just about every bottle at the bar into a mixer, mixed it up, and handed it to me with a smile. Surprisingly, it didn't taste too bad. I sipped on it till it was all gone, and then I realized why he called it "the Killer." I tried to get down off the stool and couldn't—I could not move. Everything got real fuzzy, and I was in trouble. I looked at Sam and he was fine; it didn't seem to bother him at all.

I sat there for quite a while until Sam and the rest of the guys in the band were saying, "Come on, Dewey. We've got to get back to the motel." I finally fell off the stool, and they helped me out to the hearse and threw me in, laughing all the way. I crashed at the motel and woke up just in time to shower and try to get myself together to play that night. I did play, but I had one heck of hangover just from that one drink. Needless to say, I didn't drink anymore "Killers."

Also, in Sacramento, Kent's cousin Betty came to hear us, early in the first week, and invited Kent and me to stay with her and her husband during the rest of our time there. We did, and she and her family really took good care of us, especially showing us a lot of the sights and attractions of Sacramento.

After our two weeks there, Riley booked us at the Tiger a Go-Go, located in the Hilton Inn at the San Francisco Airport. We couldn't help but notice the waitress's outfits on our first night playing, as they were exactly like the Playboy Bunny outfits. The club also had go-go dancers throughout the club, dancing in cages. It was also here that we met the group called The Fydallions, who later went on to become The Spiral Starecase and had a hit record, "More Today Than Yesterday." They were breaking down and leaving as we were coming in, and we would run into them several more times on the club circuit.

The Tiger was unique because we had a large part of the airport traffic, as well as the locals, therefore giving us a diverse amount of exposure. It was also at this time that we took a day trip into San Francisco to see the sights. We rode the cable cars, went to Chinatown, visited Candlestick Park and, finally, drove across the Golden Gate Bridge. I remember seeing Alcatraz out in the bay and was blown away by the steep hills throughout the city. It was magic, and we all loved it.

Also at the same time that we were doing these two clubs, Riley, who was always out ahead of us, was setting us up for not only more

gigs but also productions agencies and record executives. We would find all this out later in the spring, so she was still making good on her promises. After the Tiger a Go-Go at the San Francisco Airport, Riley booked us into a club in Redwood City, California, which is on the San Francisco peninsula in Northern California's Bay Area.

The club was named The Embers and was very popular in the area. We got there a couple of days early and were able to see The Fydallions perform on their last night. We, again, had followed them into a club, as we did several times on the circuit, or they were following us. This time we got to meet the guys, both at the club and motel, as they were staying at the same one we were. I remember we had several group conversations in the motel parking lot with the drummer, Vinny Parello; keyboardist, Harvey Kaye; and lead singer, Pat Upton. They were great guys, one of the best groups we saw on the circuit and very complimentary of our group. They had been on the circuit longer than us and gave us a lot of tips on what to expect at each place we played.

Vinny was another drummer who had a distinct style and great cut on his snare drum, utilizing the head and rim both on the groove, two and four, downbeat. I was also very impressed with his kick drum phrasing. He was a big influence on me changing my snare and kick drum technique that I had employed for years. Getting to know these guys and hearing them in the early days was one of the highlights of my time in California.

While we were at the club in Redwood City, we asked several of the local people who came into the club about where to go to see the popular sights and landmarks of the area. San Gregorio Beach was one of the areas that came up quite a bit as a great place to visit. We picked a day and headed to the beach; although it was still a little cool, we decided to spend a day there.

The whole band went and spent time walking along the beach, with it getting warmer as the day progressed. We came to a place where there was a large cliff area that jutted out, probably knee deep, into the water and noticed that were a lot of people on top of the cliff area looking over toward the other side. Some had binoculars and telescopes and were really focused on observing something on that side of the cliff. Curiosity got the best of all of us, so we decided to walk out around the cliff in the water to the other side to see what was going on. We got to the other side and could see people in the far distance but couldn't really figure what all the sightseers above us were interested in.

We continued up the beach, and the closer we got, we started to realize what was going on. We had walked right into a nudist colony. People were coming up to us in the nude and actually seemed quite glad to see and meet us. Now, you have to visualize, we all had bathing suits on, and some of us had tops as well, when Jon said, "What the heck" and started taking his clothes off and joined right in with them. That started a chain reaction, and before you knew it, we had all taken our clothes off and had become nudists as well.

They invited us to eat, and we spent the rest of the afternoon playing volleyball and swimming in the surf. It was all innocent, nothing sexual involved, and we had a great time getting to know the group. We later found out that this was a well-known "clothing optional" area, and we had accidentally walked right into the middle of it.

By this time we had started to realize that we really needed a home base. Russ's apartment in Hollywood had been a good temporary base, but we needed somewhere of our own. Riley informed us that we were next going to be playing in Oxnard. Oxnard was approximately 30 miles west of Los Angeles, so we started thinking that Hollywood would be a good permanent location for our home base, especially with all the plans Riley had coming up for the band.

Chapter Ten

The Carousel Club – Oxnard, California

After Redwood City, we arrived in Oxnard to begin a two-week engagement at the Carousel Club. The Carousel was a well-known club on the circuit that brought in name acts periodically, as well as the circuit bands. Located along the coast of Southern California, Oxnard is part of the larger greater Los Angeles area.

Once we were set up and started the two-week stint, Kent and I started exploring the Hollywood area for an apartment, somewhere to call home and come back to after the extended road engagements. We found an apartment on Wilton Place Boulevard, located between the Sunset and Santa Monica Boulevards. The building was brand new, with only a few occupants, and we had no trouble renting a one-bedroom apartment. The apartment was furnished, so we didn't have to worry about furniture. Shortly afterwards, the other band members rented apartments in the same building as well. The landlady was a Mrs. Noel, and she took an immediate liking to the band, especially Kent and me, as we were the first there. Everybody was paired off, with Dave and Chuk, Jon and Sam, and Riley and the girls (The Results) in their own apartments as well. This really worked well, as it was close to everything we would need in the upcoming future.

We moved in and started our nightly commutes to Oxnard. I remember the 30-mile drive took a lot longer than usual on the Los Angeles freeway due to the afternoon traffic. The drive up to Oxnard was hectic but almost deserted on the way back in the early hours of morning. When we got back to the apartment, Kent and I would sit up and watch Ralph Williams (he owned a large dealership in Van Nuys, California, and had a late night/morning television show) and eat bologna sandwiches. Our refrigerator was always stocked with bologna, as we didn't cook a lot of hot meals.

Kent and I in our apartment living room. All the furniture came with the apartment.

Kent remembered one memorable night of driving back for Jon:

"Jon had met a girl at the Carousel Club and had taken her home after we played. On the way back down to Hollywood, he pulled up to a stoplight, looked over, and noticed another really good-looking girl looking at him. He became so distracted that he took the next turn, which was wrong, got lost in the side streets and spent a couple of hours trying to find his way back to our apartment building. We laughed about that one for a long time afterward."

The apartment building was just a few blocks away from Paramount Studios, 20th Century Fox Studios and Desilu Studios, so we were right in the middle of the movie magic of Hollywood. I met a young lady at the pool who lived in the apartment building, and we became friends. She was an actress from England and was under contract to Paramount Studios. I eventually asked her out to dinner, upon which she suggested that we have it at her apartment and grill steaks on the patio.

I grilled the steaks, and when we went inside to eat I heard someone singing on the patio. We got up from the table and went to the door, and there were all the guys in the band serenading us, with their underwear pulled up over their pants, and holding the pool strainer over their heads. Sam finished it up with his signature version of "Sandman," which he added his own lyrics to. It was hilarious, and she took it well, as I explained that we were all a bunch of wild and crazy guys.

It was also during this time, at the Carousel, that Riley was busy setting us up with Steve Clark Productions in Hollywood. Steve Clark had The Association, Tommy Roe and several other name groups in his organization, Our Productions. His office was in the Sunset Towers on the corner of Sunset Boulevard and Vine. I remember going to the tower the first time, and as we were coming up to the front entrance, on ground level the doors opened with a group of people coming out. Four of the people in the group looked very familiar, and as they walked by I recognized them. It was The Mamas and Papas.

A few days later, Kent and I were on the way back to the tower to meet Riley and the guys, and as we pulled up to the light at the Sunset and Vine intersection, a convertible pulled up beside us with music

The "Action Unlimited Serenaders" on the patio

blaring loudly. We looked over and it was none other than Frank Zappa. It was not uncommon to see stars on a regular basis, out in public, especially in Hollywood.

Riley also spent time promoting the girls, The Results. They did not go out on all the engagements with us, as she had them performing in venues of their own. They did come up and sit in with us a few times at the Carousel. Chuk was dating Marti, and they spent a lot of time together.

We had several meetings with Steve Clark, and he and Riley set up our first recording session to come later in the summer. I remember during one of these meetings, Steve played the unreleased master tape of "Cherish" by The Association for us, and we all knew instantly that it was going to be a hit. We met Tommy Roe during one of those meetings and also Curt Boettcher, who worked with Steve, as his partner of Our Productions. He was to be our producer for the first record. Curt produced several hit records during his career, including "Along Comes Mary" and "Cherish" for the Association and "Sweet Pea" and "Hooray for Hazel" for Tommy Roe. He also worked with Paul Revere and the Raiders, Elton John, Gene Clark (formerly of The Byrds), The Beach Boys and other acts of the day.

At one of the meetings, we met a couple of the members of one of the big name bands in Steve's agency. They invited us to a party that night at an apartment in Hollywood. All of us in the band went, and it was quite an experience. I'm not sure whose apartment it was, but there were a lot of people there. At one point, all the furniture was pushed aside and everybody set down on the floor in a circle. Kent and I sat beside each other, and someone lit up what looked like a cigarette and started passing it around. Being the naïve Kentucky boys we were, we had not been exposed to marijuana, as it just wasn't common where we were from. As the "cigarette" got close to us, I looked at Kent and said, "What do we do?" and he replied, "I don't know." When it got to Kent, he didn't take a drag and handed it to me, and I also passed it on to the next person. After the joint was passed around, the host of the party jumped up and left, coming back holding a small white mouse in one hand and a paper bag in the other. He took a large drag off the joint, put the mouse in the bag and blew the smoke down into it. He closed the top, shook it up and then let the mouse out. The mouse commenced to run around in circles, doing flips and acrobatics that were really quite funny. The mouse was later fine, tired I'm sure, and put back in his cage. We talked and laughed about this party for months to come.

We didn't know how to smoke marijuana, as we had not been exposed to it growing up in Kentucky. Most of us in the band drank but didn't have any experience with drugs, with that being a good thing. In the months to come, we saw a lot of good bands go under from the misuse and effects of drugs. That was the first of only two times that I encountered drugs of any type the whole time we were out there.

This was an eventful two weeks, especially being brought into Steve Clark's production agency and planning for an upcoming recording session. Riley was living up to her promises to do great things for us.

Chapter Eleven

Seaside, Oxnard and Back to Vegas

Riley next booked us into a club in Seaside, California. Seaside is located northeast of Monterey on the California coast. We had a two-week engagement there, and all of us were in awe of the beauty of the area. I remember it was a small club, had good crowds and we were well received. We spent a lot of time sightseeing around the area.

One eventful day we were out sightseeing in the hearse and came up to a stoplight in downtown Seaside. Chuk was driving and Dave was in the right front seat. Kent and I were in the back, sitting on the side, looking out the side window. When we stopped at the light, a car pulled up beside us. The guy driving, and I presume his girlfriend, were laughing and pointing at the hearse and us in it. I thought since they were laughing at us that I would give them something to laugh about, so I mooned them. We pulled out as the light turned and, of course, Dave and Chuk, who were in front, had no idea what had happened. A few blocks up, we were pulled over by a policeman, and again, Chuk didn't know why he was pulled over. The policeman started by saying, "A funeral hearse was reported driving around town with naked people in the back." Dave and Chuk immediately looked at Kent and I, knowing that we were the guilty parties. Chuk recalled:

"Four of us got out of the hearse, and would you believe the couple couldn't identify who had mooned them! He let us go for lack of evidence. I almost wrecked when we started back out from laughing so hard."

I think that was the last time we mooned anyone, as we had learned our lesson.

I met a girl at the club early on during the Seaside engagement and became good friends with her during the time there. When we finished up, on the last Saturday night, she wanted to go back to Hollywood with me. I told her that I couldn't take her because we were on the road so much and it would be impossible. She was relentless and finally told me that, if I didn't take her, she would kill herself. I didn't take her seriously, and after we had packed up the final piece of equipment in the panel truck, someone in the parking lot yelled, "There's a girl on the edge of the roof!" Just as I looked around, I heard and saw someone hitting the top of one of the cars in the parking lot. It was her. We all ran over, and she was alive but in great pain. Someone called for an ambulance; the medics arrived, loaded her up and left. All the way back down to Hollywood, I was really worried, feeling responsible for what had happened.

Riley booked us back into the Carousel Club in Oxnard for another two-week stint. So, we were back to the nightly commute. After we were settled back into the apartment a few days later, I heard the doorbell ring one afternoon and answered the door to see a girl in a full upper body cast, with her right arm being held upward by a metal rod, supporting herself with a cane with the other arm/hand. It was the girl from Seaside. I let her in and found out that she had somehow learned where we lived in Hollywood, came down with her sister and was staying in a motel close by. Kent was there as well and in shock at the sight of her. I felt much better that she was okay, alive and well, although in a full body cast. I spent the whole afternoon trying to convince her that this was not going to work and that she could not stay. Her sister agreed with me and helped me to convince her to go back to her home in Portland, Oregon to heal. We parted on good terms, and I was really glad that she was okay but never found out how she located us.

We were starting our second appearance at The Carousel club in Oxnard when, on Monday of that week, the owner informed us that he had Billy Preston and The Newbeats coming in on Tuesday night and that we would be backing them.

We knew Billy Preston from seeing him on *Shindig!* He was already a legendary session musician, having backed Little Richard, Sam Cooke and Ray Charles. Later, his solo career featured hit singles such as "That's the Way God Planned It," "Outa-Space," Will It Go Round In Circles," "Space Race" and "Nothing from Nothing." He is also remembered for performing with The Beatles on "Get Back" during the famous concert on the rooftop of Abbey Road Studio in London, as featured in the film *Let It Be*.

The Newbeats were a vocal trio who had a number 2 hit in 1964 with "Bread and Butter." They had followed that with three more singles, the most popular being "Run, Baby Run (Back Into My Arms)," which made it to number 12 in 1965.

The owner of the Carousel usually set aside Tuesday nights as the night for bringing top name acts in, and we were fortunate to be there when he brought these two in. We didn't have much time to prepare for either, from finding out Monday to backing them on Tuesday, but we were quite excited and started our research immediately. We met both acts early Tuesday afternoon for a rehearsal and were really impressed at how nice and easy they were to work with. When we did the show that night to a packed house, The Newbeats went on first and we had no problems backing them, with all going well. I remember how much fun it was doing "Bread and Butter" with them as that was the only song that I sang with AU. I'm not really a singer, but I could do the high falsetto and therefore was elected to sing that part.

Then, Billy Preston came on, playing Sam's Hammond B3 and Leslie system, and he rocked the house. At rehearsal with him that afternoon, he did the song "Summertime" with the whole band and wowed us all. When it came time to do it in his show, he had all the band leave the stage except me. All he wanted was the drums backing him up. So, there I was on stage with just Billy Preston. I was very nervous but made it through the song fine, and to this day, that is the number one highlight of my entire drumming career. I can truly say that I performed on stage with Billy Preston, just the two of us. I know, in reality, that it would not have mattered who the drummer was, but it was a big thrill and lifetime memory for me. Actually, the entire band was thrilled to perform on stage with Preston, as it was a career highlight for all of them, as well.

After the show, we invited both Preston and the Newbeats to our apartment in Hollywood to party with us the rest of the night and morning. They accepted and came down with us. We had a great time with both. I don't think I've ever met anyone as nice and humble as Billy Preston, and I followed his career for years after that.

When we finished up at the Carousel, Riley booked us at the Pussycat a Go-Go in Las Vegas. We were going back to Vegas for the second time.

Opening in 1964, the Pussycat a Go-Go was the first rock 'n' roll nightclub in Vegas. The Pussycat soon became "the place" to hang out

Kent and me outside the Carousel Club in Oxnard, California. Notice the tiger skin jacket, and boots, Kent is holding and the turtle neck and black pants I have on. That was the outfit described before. We were packing up (bass drum in background) to leave for our second appearance in Las Vegas. Riley had booked us into the Pussy Cat A Go-Go on the strip in Vegas.

and was regularly frequented by headline acts from the casinos after their show was over. The club became the place for musicians, showgirls, dealers, and others to party, with dancing until 8 a.m.

I remember how hot it was driving into Las Vegas in June. The heat was much more intense than it was the first time. Of course, then it was late winter and the weather was pleasant, but what a change. We also found out at the club that we were going on at 12 a.m. and playing at one-hour intervals, quitting at 8 a.m. The Pussycat had two stages, which meant that two bands were playing, one after the other switching each hour, so there was constant music. We would play an hour, the other band would play an hour, and so forth. So, our schedule was midnight till 1 a.m., 2 till 3, 4 till 5 and finally 6 till 7., with the other band playing on till 8 a.m. It was a grueling schedule but always fun, as the club was packed all through the early morning hours.

I also got to see my brother again and spend time with him. We again took some more day trips, seeing all the sights around the Las Vegas area. Mostly during the days we were sleeping because of the club hours that we had to play.

We also got to see The Checkmates during that time. We saw them the first time in L.A. and always tried to catch their show if they were anywhere close to where we were. They had one of the best floor shows we had ever seen. I think we later modeled our floor shows after theirs. The Checkmates were one of Las Vegas's top lounge acts and also performed at the Pussycat a Go-Go. They had a number 13 hit in the U.S. in 1969, "Black Pearl."

The Pussycat was much different from the Thunderbird, as it was more of a dance-oriented Club whereas the Thunderbird was a lounge concert type of setting. There were many nights there that we wondered if we were going to make it through due to being so tired. Chuk recalled:

"It was a double stage, opposite each other, with us trading off with another band. I don't remember if we traveled just before we played there, but the off-and-on sets took a toll. I think it was the second or third set when Dave called for 'Barefootin'. The song starts with a guitar intro, and then the band kicks in. I played the intro, and then I remembered snapping awake as my knees began to buckle. I turned to Kent and said, "I think I just fell asleep!" Kent said, "You can't have fallen asleep. You've been playing the whole time." Problem was, we were into the second verse by then, and I hadn't missed a note. Kent didn't believe me, but by the next set, it was happening to him, too."

The acoustics were really strange in the club, with the drums sounding really muffled, or like cardboard. Chuk also recalled:

"That club had a sound-absorbing wallpaper with about a 1/8-inch or 1/4-inch foam padding beneath it. Those were the strangest acoustics I had ever heard. I don't know what song it was, but Dewey did a roll from the upper toms to the lower toms and busted out laughing when he heard it himself."

The main thing I remember about the Pussycat was that it was a great club, fun experience, very hot at that time of year, and it was great to get to see my brother again. We finished the two weeks, with Riley letting us know that we were heading back to Hollywood to start our recording session. We were very excited and couldn't wait to get back. Again, Riley was coming through on her promises.

Chapter Twelve

Recording First Record

Coming back to Hollywood this time was more exciting than the previous times. We were going to cut our first record, and that was a big thrill for us. Riley informed us that Steve Clark had booked us into Columbia Studios in Hollywood for our session and that Curt Boettcher would be producing. We knew that Curt had produced records for The Association, as well as Tommy Roe and other name artists.

We also had a couple of weeks off from the road, so we could concentrate on the two songs for the record. Chuk had already been collaborating with Riley on writing the two songs so that we would be ready when we went in. We spent the first couple of days in Steve's office, and it was here and then that we found out we would not be playing the music ourselves. Chuk remembered:

"What I remember is that we had a recording session scheduled with Steve Clark, like on a Monday in L.A. Riley was worried about not having any songs for the session. I wrote both songs (on a weekend previously while we were on the road) and we went right in and recorded with Steve and Curt's studio musicians. The difference was that, in the L.A. studio, those guys did their own arrangement for the song after listening to me play it a couple of times (actually, probably after hearing it once)."

The rest of us were disheartened that we would not be playing the music, but we found out that week that this was the standard procedure, since the studio musicians could do the tracks in a fraction of the time it would take us. This was done for most all of the bands, especially with the big studios, and still is when you're on the road and cannot spend time in the studios. There were several studio bands that recorded music for name bands, with the most famous being L.A.'s The Wrecking Crew. Kent and I were especially let down as we wanted to play on our first national record, but it was not to be.

At one time during those first couple of days we were in Sunset Towers, and we had gone to get some lunch. On the way back up on the elevator, we met the leader of the studio musician group on his way up to Steve Clark's office. I don't remember his name, but he was telling us about how much he liked our songs. He also reassured us that using studio musicians was a commonly accepted practice and to not let it affect us, as we would have a lot to do on the vocal recordings coming up next.

After the meetings with Riley and Steve during the first of the week, I remember going to Columbia Studios for the next step, to record the vocals. We had seen the Columbia Studio building many times in Hollywood, not realizing that we would actually be recording a record there. The building itself was huge, with individual studio rooms everywhere, and I found myself wondering how many hit records and artists had been through here before us. Once we got settled into our particular studio, we found out that it was the one that Percy Faith recorded in, as well. I'm sure many other famous artists had recorded there also, and we were as star-struck as we were the first week we arrived in Hollywood.

We met Curt and he explained all the procedures we would be going through, along with using some of the same background vocalists that were on the Association records. Sam would sing the lead on the A side, with Chuk singing the lead on the B side, with the rest of the band providing harmonies along with the background singers. I remember there were two rooms in the studio, one with theater type seating and the other with all the microphones, baffles, etc. The wall between the two had a huge window glass so that you could see from one into the other. The lead vocals were done first, and I remember sitting in the room with the seats watching both Sam and Chuk in the other room with their headsets on doing the leads. After the leads were done, it was time for the background harmonies. The extra background singers came in to assist, and the harmonies were added to the final tracks.

We spent a few days doing both sides, and when the vocals were finished, Curt added a strange "special effect intro" to the A side that we had not heard before and didn't know it was going to be on the song. Chuk remembered:

"When we did 'My Heart Cries Out,' it was originally a two verses-chorus-third verse song, and I was in on the mixing session where Curt changed all that. I didn't hear the special effects he did until later (he used the vocal harmony tracks to create those sounds), but I remember he edited the song to fit the time frame he wanted. They cut and spliced the tape, and if you listen closely, the bass does a slide from a low E and goes up, only instead of landing on the higher E, it actually ends on the low E again because that's where the splice was made. Today, those things would be easy, but then it was Curt Boettcher creating something that hadn't been done before. I have to say, I never liked the 'psychedelic' bit he did to the song, but I had no more to say about it than anyone else did. Anyway, when we cut the vocals for 'Thinking To Myself' (which should have been the A-side until Curt did what he did to the other song) in Columbia studios, Curt wanted an instrumental solo in the middle. I ran down to the music store on the corner of Sunset and Vine and bought a harmonica, went right back into the studio and recorded it. I was the only one in AU who played an instrument on that record, strangely enough."

I remember that all of us in the group were not pleased with the psychedelic effect, but it was explained to us that it would be a good "hook" as rock music was starting to go through a big change and this would help the song appeal to a broader audience. It was really strange because we were more of a horn-oriented R&B and Soul type of band. Sam's lead on "My Heart Cries Out" displayed his soulful voice and the record was perfectly crafted, with the best producer and studio in the business, but we were really concerned that it really was not who we were. Riley comforted us by explaining that we had the best in the business behind us and not to worry. She was right, as we had just cut a record at Columbia Studios within fewer than six months of leaving Kentucky and we had a lot to look forward to.

We did all of the recording on the two songs during the day, which gave us the nights off. We spent a couple of nights exploring the nightclubs of the Sunset Strip with the most memorable being The Whisky a Go-Go and Hullabaloo. Both clubs had top names acts appearing on a regular basis, including Smokey Robinson and the Miracles, The Leaves, Sir Douglas Quintet and Freddie Cannon. It was fun to go see other acts, especially top-name acts, as the Strip was full of them. We finished up the two-week period at Columbia Studios being very excited about our future. The next step would be for Steve Clark to market the master to record companies, hoping for a major label to be interested. It would be a few weeks before we would know who bought the master and when it would be released. We also found out that our next gig was in Fresno, California.

Fresno is in the center of the San Joaquin Valley, approximately 220 miles northwest of Los Angeles. We arrived in mid-summer to play at a club named The Place.

The club was owned by Ron Pearson, who was a musician and leader of the house band, Ron Pearson and The Ron Dons. The club was situated outside of town and was very popular in the area, having large crowds nightly. I remember the stage was in the middle on the back wall with a large dance floor, with table seating areas to the right, middle and left of the stage.

The motel we stayed at was very close by and had a restaurant that served great steaks, giving us all we needed for the two-week engagement. We got there in time to catch Ron and his band performing on the last night before a planned two-week vacation. It was very hot, so we spent a lot of daylight hours at the motel pool.

I also remember working up the Sam and Dave song, "Hold On I'm Coming," while we were in Fresno. Sam McIntosh sang the lead, being the true soul singer in our group. Dave Osborn was a great arranger and that turned out to be one of our signature cover songs. The real Sam and Dave—Mr. Moore and Mr. Prater—would have been proud of our version.

Playing at The Place was also my first experience with a double bass drum kit. Ron Pearson's drummer played a double bass kit and offered to leave them set up for me to play. I played them the first night we were there but found myself being "way too busy" with the extra bass drum. I set my single bass kit up the following day, being very appreciative of the experience. It was fun playing his kit, but I really preferred the single bass setup.

We also took a great day trip to Santa Clara to ride the sand dunes in special dune buggies owned by a group of friends we met at the club. We spent the whole day riding up and down sand dunes in a roller coaster technique. We were worn out and sore when we got back late that afternoon. I'm not sure how we played that night, but we did with Sam and Jon barely able to make it up onto the stage.

Another eventful trip the band made was to the Fresno Zoo. We were at the monkey cage, which was quite large and above the sidewalk level. There were several playful chimps that seemed to love our attention. Dave was having fun mocking one and tantalizing him, not having any idea that the chimp was very smart and on to him. He kept it up, and the chimp finally had enough. There were several piles of chimp feces on the ground of the cage, and you could tell the chimp had something on his mind because he was sizing Dave up pretty good. He took off running, making a loud screeching sound, reaching down with his hand, gathering a substantial amount of feces, and slinging it. The chimp hit a perfect bullseye on the front of Dave's yellow shirt. It's almost like he had practiced that shot daily as it was perfectly placed. Dave was shocked, as he was a very neat dresser and prided himself on his appearance. We were all laughing so hard that all the other chimps started mocking us so loudly that you could hear it throughout the entire zoo.

We had to cut our zoo trip short so Dave could get back to the motel for a change of clothing. We made a few trips back to the zoo, but Dave

Deejay copy of "My Heart Cries Out"

never agitated the chimps again. Every time I've visited a zoo since that day, I've always thought of him, his chimp friend and stained yellow shirt. We made a lot of good friends in Fresno, some that followed us to other parts of California to see us play. I think that chimp would have followed Dave, if he could have, just to mess up his day.

During the second week in Fresno, we received word from Riley and Steve Clark that Mercury Records and Cameo-Parkway were very interested in our master. Just before we left, Riley called to tell us that Cameo Parkway Records might outbid Mercury.

Cameo-Parkway was a big company, so that was good news. Based in Philadelphia, they released records under both the Cameo and Parkway labels and had a very cozy relationship with Dick Clark and *American Bandstand*. Some of the label's top artists included Bobby Rydell, Chubby Checker, The Dovells (featuring Len Barry as lead singer), The Orlons, Dee Dee Sharp, and The Tymes. Riley seemed to think that Cameo would buy the master, giving us great hope that we might be on a major label before the year was out. Eventually, Cameo Parkway did buy the master a few weeks later, and we heard talk of a fall 1966 release nationally. Riley was again coming through with her promises of big things for the group.

Chapter Thirteen

Drum Lessons, Draft Boards and Portland

I also worked out time, during the summer of '66, to get down to San Diego to meet and study under Riley's friend, the drummer who I mentioned before. His name was Giovanni DiSimone. He owned a music store and was also a member of the San Diego Symphony.

On our first meeting, he had me demonstrate my sticking technique, immediately recognizing the bad habits I had developed since my lessons with Cecil Jones back in Kentucky. He praised the basics that Cecil had taught me but started me back on a strong regiment of rudiments and exercises that I had gotten away from. He gave me a drum pad, took a quarter out of his pocket, held it in the middle of the pad, drew a circle around it and told me to never let the tips of the sticks get outside of the circle. (I still have that pad, and you can still see the circle after years of practicing). I was playing traditional grip then, and he corrected the stick position in my left hand from the middle of the third finger down to the tip to give me more rebound. It was very painful and bloody at first, but I eventually built up a callous, which gave me much more freedom, as I had been gripping the stick too tightly before. He was very patient with me, and I made it down to San Diego every chance I could to study with him.

It was also during that summer that I really started realizing the hardships of being on the road. We had motel, food, and laundry bills from every place we played, as well as clothing and equipment purchases. If we were lucky enough to find motels that had kitchenettes we would cook our own meals, but mostly we had to survive by eating in restaurants. The motels, normally, would give us discounts because of our extended stays, as playing on the club circuit usually required that you spend a couple of weeks at each engagement. Our band uniform was suits and ties, and you could sweat completely through them in one night, which created a pretty hefty laundry bill. You had to budget your money and plan ahead, as all those things could get quite expensive.

Our equipment developed lots of wear and tear from all the loading, unloading, and setups, so it seemed like you were always having to replace something. One of the first things we did when we came into a new gig was to find the local music store and head there as soon as we could. We also developed a band "kitty" of funds that we all donated to out of every paycheck to cover our gas and vehicle expenses.

It was exciting being on the road, but in reality, it was also very expensive. I wasn't very good at planning or budgeting, so Kent kept me going by helping to manage my money and budget. He was very mature, a good planner and a good friend. Looking back on those days, I don't know how I would have made it without his guidance and help. I was not nearly as mature or forward thinking as Kent, especially on finances.

One thing that was on all our minds was the draft, as Vietnam was escalating, and this was very scary for the whole band. Here we were right on the verge of taking the band to a much higher level, and losing any one member could be catastrophic. We were all at the prime ages to be called up. We had a tremendous chemistry in the band, with six members who played and got along great with each other. There were no egos. Everyone was a team member and worked hard to make the group successful. To lose anyone from that team would definitely disrupt the chemstry. I have to say that none of us were unpatriotic, but to be inducted into the service at this time, especially with the band on the verge of making it big, would have been terrible timing. This would really change the band later in the fall of '66.

Another event for the band would come in the summer of '66. Chuk and Marti, one of the female singers of the duo "The Results," had been dating since we arrived in California. Marti became pregnant and was due in the fall, so she and Chuk decided not to get married with all the activity coming up for the band. Vicki and Marti had been working with Riley throughout the spring and summer promoting their own group and they felt, due to Marti's pregnancy, that it would be better for them to return to Cincinnati to have the baby and possibly return at a later time. This was a hard decision and tough for all of us as we had become very close to the girls and been through a lot with them the past several months. They returned to Ohio later in the summer, and Marti had a baby girl in the fall.

The girls did not return to California but performed for the next several years throughout Ohio and Kentucky. They were very popular in later years performing at several Lexington clubs, including The Rebel Room and the Terrace Room.

Also during that summer, we had a new promotional picture taken of the band. Riley was working with the Gail McConkey Booking Agency, and Gail scheduled us for a new band picture. I remember we took the picture at her agency in Los Angeles, and she scheduled it during one of the nights that we were recording our record at Columbia Studios.

The picture was a much different look than the first one taken when we first arrived in California. We had matured a lot, and Gail wanted a much more sophisticated look for the band. Our band uniform had changed from the bell bottom pants, puffed sleeve shirts, and boots to black suits, white shirts, and either silver or black ties. This was our standard club uniform, mainly because most of the clubs we played were upper level and we had to look the part. I remember that the picture shoot was somewhat uncomfortable because the photographer wanted us to lean into each other with a strong tilt to our right sides. The picture turned out great, but our legs were killing us due to the leaning position. Kent and Dave, both being taller than me, were in the front row and were not only having to lean but stoop down as well, making it even more uncomfortable. We had a lot of fun doing the shoot and the picture turned out great.

Riley next booked us in Portland, Oregon after our recording sesson in L.A., which was the farthest north we had been on the West Coast. The drive up was very scenic, with the surrounding area around Portland being beautiful. The weather was a little cooler in the Portland area, and I remember there was a lot of rain.

We would be playing at the Town Mart club, which was just out of the downtown area on the outskirts of the city. This booking was for a month, which was the longest so far of all the other engagements we had worked. When we arrived and were setting up on stage the first day, someone yelled from the bar area, “Phone call for Dewey Pope!” This was strange because I didn’t know anyone in Portland, or thought I didn’t. I answered, and it was the girl from Seaside, California. Remember her, the girl on the roof? It hit me immediately that she was from Portland and had found out that we would be playing there. She wanted to come hear us and I told her it was fine, later wondering if that was the right thing to do.

The Town Mart was a fairly large club with a semi-circular stage on the right rear wall. It had a large dance floor with seating all around and back to the bar. This was the club that we would use to start doing our "floor shows." We had discussed doing a floor show quite a bit, and being in this club for a longer period would give us time to work one up and try out on the audience. We remembered how much we liked The Checkmates' floor shows, so that gave us a model to go by.

We decided that Jon would be our choreographer, as he had always been the leader of our previous antics on stage and was also the designated Master of Ceremonies for the group. He had some great ideas, and we knew it would be fun to add these to our regular stage performances. Some of Jon's previous antics on stage included announcing to the audience that the next song we would do "stinks" and he and the rest of guys up front would then put gas masks on. He did the James Brown routine, with the cape being put over him at the song's ending, and he would fling it off and continue back into the song, with this going on several times before the song actually ended. He also did a great routine to the song "House of The Rising Sun." A lot of our fun on stage would be pranks on each other. Chuk recalls a prank on Dave in Portland:

"We had a strong following there and pretty much *carte blanche* to do anything we liked. I remember they described us as a 'six-way tennis match' because any one of us could and would be doing something spontaneously. Anyway, Dave had gotten a valve trombone to augment his trumpet work. I don't remember which song it was on, but he played trumpet on part of it, then always reached behind himself to pick up the trombone for a quick switch. I had both hands occupied playing guitar, so I used a straw to suck up water from a glass onstage and leaned over to expel the water into the trombone mouthpiece, this being done behind Dave's back, but obviously in full view of the audience. I nearly had it filled it when Dave reached back for it as I stepped aside. He put the trombone to his lips and blew (with a very puzzled look on his face). He knew something was wrong, but he blew anyway. At first there was nothing, until a huge spout of water sprayed the unsuspecting dancers below us. I don't know if it was good for the horn, but it was definitely good for a laugh."

I remember that we had so much fun on stage that it infected the audience as well. I think we stretched the limit on our antics in Portland. We had stage props that included a Hoss Cartwright hat, gas masks, smoking jackets and empty guitar cases. I remember one night the prank was on me.

We were playing a song, and someone came over and put the Hoss Cartwright hat on my head. The hat was very big and literally came down over my eyes and ears so that I couldn't see anything at all. My drums were set up on the right side of the stage and everybody snuck off, leaving me there playing on alone. Chuk and Kent must have had long enough cords to keep playing because I did not pick up on what was happening in my "blinded" state. When I did finally realize what was going on, I went into an extended drum solo and the crowd loved it. I think they thought it was planned, but it wasn't. There was another routine where the guys on the front line of the group would play the guitar cases with their gas masks on.

The "Spontaneous Factor" was one of the things that made the group so great, the ability of any one of us to be showmen on our own. The Town Mart gave us the opportunity to not only grow as musicians but also to expand and tweak our showmanship on stage. We did work up our first actual floor show, where Dave put on a smoking jacket, adding a pipe and glass of wine to play an effeminate English gentleman. In the days before political correctness, we called this "The Figouro Fag Routine."

Sam interviewed him as if he was on a television show. Dave had a perfect English accent and it went over well. I always felt that Dave had missed his calling and should have been an actor, as he was great at it. We worked up a couple more shows and had lots of fun, both between ourselves and the audience doing them.

The girl from Seaside did show up on the first night but directed all her attention to Jon instead of me. By this time she was totally healed. She and I became good friends for the rest of our time there. Jon dated her several times but nothing came of it.

There was a liquor store beside the club and one night, after the club had shut down, Jon and Sam went over to get a drink at the store. They ended up meeting several people inside and stayed there the rest of the night drinking. One of the guys they met was a truck driver, who told them that he had to make a run up to Seattle the next day and would

Dave doing his "English Gentleman" and "Elvis" skits

be back in time for them to play that night. He offered to take them up with him so they could see Seattle. They, being a little drunk at the time, accepted and rode up with him. Jon recalls:

"I immediately passed out in the back of the truck, and when we got there, he woke me up to see the Space Needle. I woke up, looked at it out the window, said 'okay' and passed back out. I don't remember a lot about my first trip to Seattle, as I slept most of the day. When we left going back to Portland, I knew we were not going to make it by 9 p.m. so I called Riley and told her to bring both Sam's and my band clothes to the club and we would dress there. We finally made it in with all the band anxiously awaiting us, got dressed, and was on the stage by 10 p.m. The band played the first set without us. We didn't do any more late night or early morning trips to the liquor store next door after that."

Dave also received his first draft notice while we were in Portland. We were in the motel, in Dave's room, and someone knocked on the door. When we answered there was a man in a black suit with an envelope in his hand. He asked if there was a Dave Osborn there; we said yes, with Dave coming to the door and taking the envelope. The man left and upon opening it, Dave discovered it was his draft notice. All of our moods changed to disbelief, as the reality of one of us being called up was finally happening. The report date was several weeks away, and we knew we would not be in Portland then, so Riley was going to notify the board and let them know where we would be so he could report there, wherever that might be. Kent, Jon and I had already reported to the draft boards in Kentucky and California but had not received any further notices. I remember that it dwelled on us for the next few days, but we wanted to put it out of our minds, especially with the record coming out, but little did we know then of what was to come a few months later.

We built a great following in Portland and made some really good friends—one in particular was Doug Crombie. Doug was from Portland and a guitar player as well. He came to hear us quite often and sat in with us several times. We actually made him an honorary seventh member of the band. We also had friends in Portland who followed us throughout the West Coast.

On our way up to Portland, we went by Mount Shasta and noticed that there was a national park there as well. I think the city close by was also named Shasta. After we had been in Portland a couple of weeks, Chuk and I developed an interest in diving and started renting scuba equipment. We practiced using the equipment in the motel pool and got fairly proficient with it and started planning a trip back down to Shasta, as there was a large lake there, and Riley had some business there to take care of as well. Chuk remembered:

"I can't tell you how many times time I've thought about that trip and the pontoon we rented. It triggers another memory—that being the reason we went down there from Portland, I believe, was to pick up either the hearse or Caddy that had been worked on. It was you, me, and Riley, I think." (The "Caddy" was a 1953 Cadillac Sedan that we picked up after arriving in California.)

We planned the trip, with Riley, on one of our nights off, leaving early in the morning, spending the night and coming back the next day. We rented a pontoon boat, went out on the lake and spent the day diving in the clear waters.

The water was very clear, and we could see quite a bit but found out quickly that you can lose your bearings very easily under water. I remember we dived and swam to the shore and started back out to the pontoon boat directly in front of us. When we thought we were at the boat, we surfaced and saw that we were in the dock area, which was to our extreme right from where we started. There were boats motoring all around us, and needless to say, the dock owner was very upset, mainly for our safety, and I don't blame him. From that point on, we dived under and around the pontoon boat, not attempting any more long swims underwater.

The time in Portland was eventful. The group was changing but in a good way, especially with the addition of the floor shows. Also, at the end of our month-long stay, Riley informed us that Cameo Parkway would be releasing our record nationally in October. Again, she was coming through with her promises. The only negative in Portland was Dave's first draft notice, but we were so excited with the record news that we put it aside and didn't think about it.

Chapter Fourteen

Back to Fresno – *Shindig!* – San Francisco – Utah

After the month-long engagement in Portland, Riley booked us back into the club in Fresno, The Place, that we had played earlier in the summer. During the two weeks that we were there, Kent and I had decided to close out the apartment in Hollywood, as we had hardly been there at all in the past few months. We took a day off and traveled back down to L.A. and closed the apartment out. The rest of the band eventually did the same, as we were spending so much time out on the road that it wasn't practical to keep the expenses of an apartment up. We also visited Kent's uncle in Riverside and spent the night with him. Kent also bought a car while we were there, a 1953 Chrysler, and we left it with his uncle to pick up at a later date.

After the two weeks in Fresno, Riley booked us back in the Carousel Club in Oxnard. We really liked the Carousel and had a great following there, only this time we stayed at a motel in the area, as we had closed out the apartment in Hollywood. Steve, the owner, was still doing the Celebrity Tuesday nights and had booked the Count Basie Orchestra in during our first week there. Count Basie's drummer at that time was Louie Bellson, and I was as taken with him as I was back in my early days of watching Bud Ecton. He played a double bass kit, which was not common for most drummers in those days.

Louie Bellson was not only a composer, arranger and bandleader, but he was also an innovator, credited with being the first to use two bass drums. He was a vice-president of Remo drum company and also happened to be married to legendary actress and jazz singer Pearl Bailey.

I sat on the front row, star-struck and totally captivated with his playing. After the show, all I could talk about was Louie Bellson. Little did I know that I had a big surprise waiting for me the next night when we pulled into the club parking lot. Evidently, the owner had overheard me talking about Bellson, so he, with the rest of the band's knowledge, "doctored" the outside club marquee to say, "Dewey Belson Pope Featuring Action Unlimited."

All night long, people were giving me a hard time with some even saying, "Who is Dewey Belson Pope?" It was a thrill to see Count Basie, his orchestra, and especially Louie Bellson, but I had no idea that it would become a lifetime memory, thanks to Steve and the rest of the band.

Another event for us while we were in Oxnard was doing a *Shindig!* show for the USO in Long Beach, California. The gig would be at the Navy Shipyard and would be hosted by Jimmy O'Neil, the host of the television show *Shindig!*, a musical variety series that ran in the mid-'60s on ABC. The show featured the biggest pop and rock acts of the day. The house band—The Shindogs—featured Glen Campbell, Billy Preston, Leon Russell and others who went on to become household names.

This particular show would not be televised but would have all the full features of the show, with us being the headliner. We picked Jimmy O'Neil up in L.A., and he rode down with us to Long Beach in the hearse. I remember he was very nice to all of us and joked a lot about going to a gig in the back of a hearse.

We did the show on a huge stage out in the open part of the shipyard, with an audience full of sailors. Riley's husband, Russ, was retired from the U.S. Navy, and before the concert, he took all of us on a tour of one of the ships and the area around the shipyard. It was very interesting and quite busy, as I'm sure the war in Vietnam had a lot to do with that. We had so much going on with the band that we didn't think much about Vietnam, but it was very much in the news every night. I remember talking to several Vietnam veterans at the Carousel Club during breaks about their experiences in the war. The show, and especially Jimmy O'Neil, was well received, with us spending quite a bit of time with the sailors after the show. They were very appreciative of our taking the time to perform for them.

It was also during this time at the Carousel that I had my second encounter with marijuana. We had played the first set of the night, and on the break, I went back to the dressing room. One of the club regulars who we had become friends with came back and offered us a smoke. Now you have to remember, I didn't have any experience at all with drugs in Kentucky, but I had heard lots about marijuana since we first landed in California so I decided to try a hit. I did, inhaling

Hickman Elementary School, where I caught the drumming bug in 1957

The original Monzzas. L-R: Paul Wasson (bass guitar), C.B. Spicer (saxophone), Kent Fox (lead guitar), Gary Spencer (lead singer) and Dewey Pope (drums). This picture was taken in Kent's father's photography studio in 1963.

The Exiles, 1964. Clockwise from top: Buzz Cornelison, Mike Howard, Jimmy Stokley, Paul Smith Jr., Mack Davenport, and Billy Luxon. Courtesy of Mack Davenport.

The Impressions (early Maroons). Front row: Jimmy "Hutch" Hutcherson, John Moore, Chuck Campbell. Second row: George Ridings, Ray Linville, Larry Joe True and Bob Becker. This group was playing at Speck's during 1961 and 1962. (www.Speck'sEKUAlumni.com)

The Maroons, 1964. Front row: Jon Anderson, Bill Rauth and Larry Joe True. Back row: George Ridings, Gary Edwards, Dave Osborn and Tom Colgan. (www.Speck'sEKUAlumni.com)

Action Unlimited, 1965. Front row, L-R: Jerry Morse, Dave Osborn, Sam McIntosh. Back row: Chuk Trisko, Jon Anderson and Kent Fox.

Riley Kincaid, manager of Action Unlimited, 1966

Action Unlimited publicity photo, shot at Griffith Park, Hollywood, California, 1966. From left to right, back row: Kent Fox, Jon Anderson, Dewey Pope, Sam McIntosh and Chuk Trisko. Sitting in front on the boulder is Dave Osborn. Dave and Sam used their stage names of "Sammy Mack" and "David Lee Baines".

Dewey, Chuck, Dave and Sam at the motel

Marquee at The Place in Fresno promoting our appearance, summer 1966

Publicity photo, summer 1966

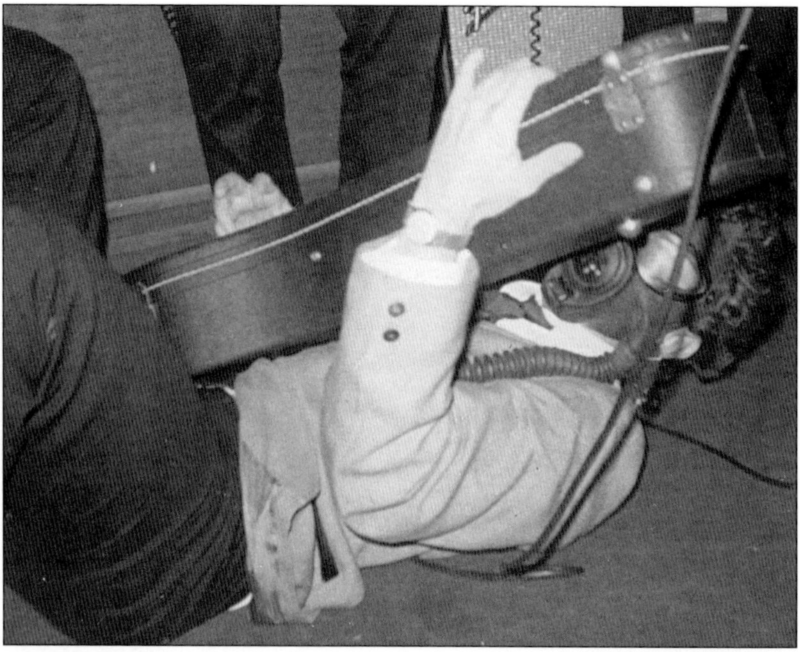

Clowning around on stage in Portland

Jon doing one of his many routines

Dave "The Director" conducting the "Action Unlimited Orchestra"

Action Unlimited on stage at the Town Mart in Portland, Oregon

Marquee at the Carousel Club in Oxnard, California, inspired by my adulation of jazz drummer Louie Bellson

Action Unlimited publicity photo, 1967

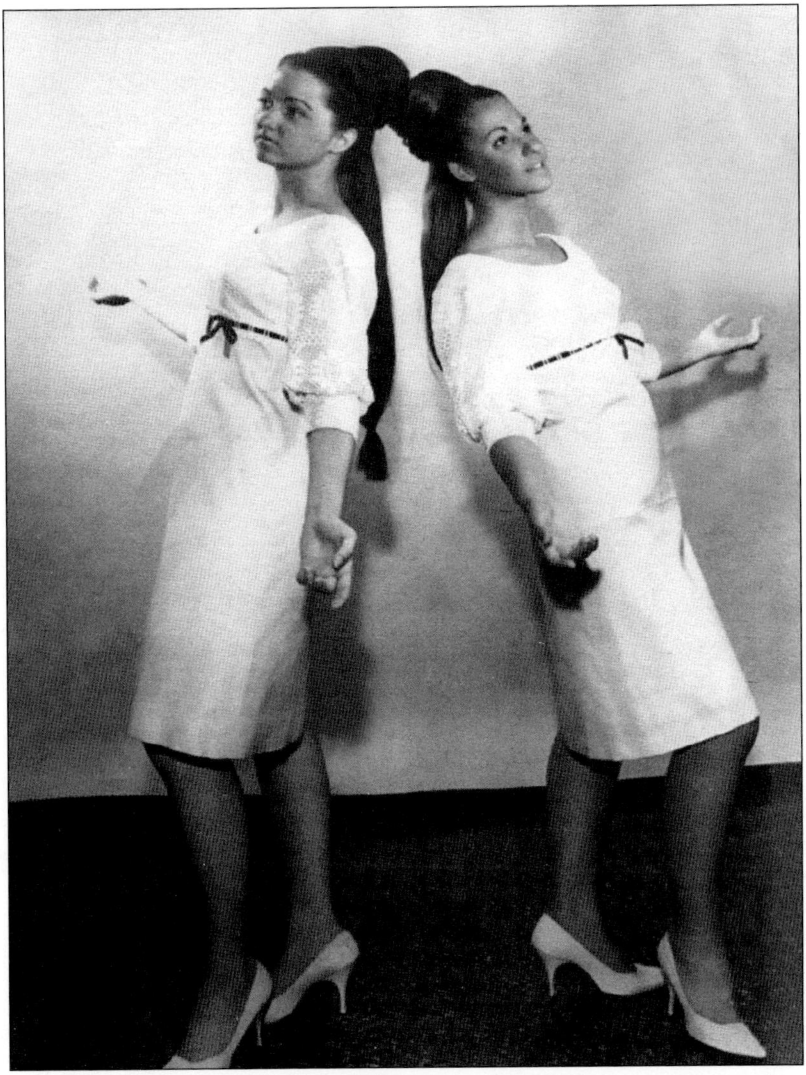

The Results—Vicki and Marti Jones, 1965

Sam takes a break from his keyboards to perform as the lead guitarist during a performance at The Town Mart, Portland, Oregon.

I put down the sticks to don a gas mask on during our "This Song Stinks" routine at The Town Mart, Portland, Oregon.

Jon swaps his sax for a microphone as he sings at The Town Mart, Portland, Oregon.

Kent on stage in our signature tiger skin jacket at the Red Velvet, Hollywood, California

Kent and Sam make faces for the camera on stage at the Carousel Club, Oxnard, California.

Jon performing "House of the Rising Sun" at The Town Mart, Portland, Oregon

Me clowning for the camera on stage at the Carousel Club, Oxnard, California

Since Kent sat on my riser, I decided to use his head as a drum during a practice session at The Place Club in Fresno, California..

Jon enjoys a break during one of our performances in Ogden, Utah.

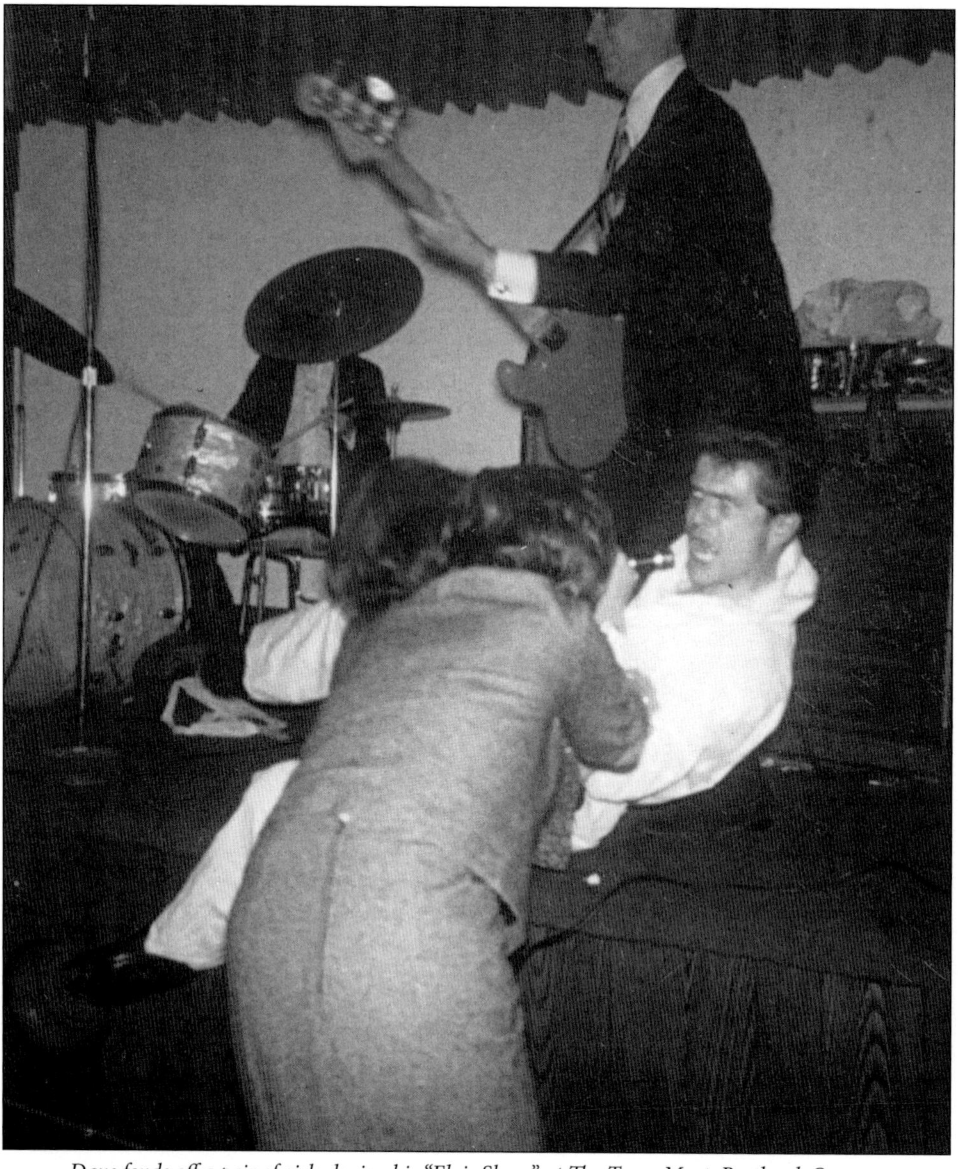

Dave fends off a pair of girls during his "Elvis Show" at The Town Mart, Portland, Oregon.

Chuk (center) takes a turn as lead singer on stage at The Town Mart, Portland, Oregon, flanked by Dave (left) and Kent.

Kent and Chuk work some choreography into the act at The Town Mart, Portland, Oregon.

Kent switching off to sing lead with Dave on bass at the Town Mart, Portland, Oregon

The band and I got "TP'd" during one of our floor shows in Ogden, Utah.

Me on stage at IJ's in Palm Springs, California

Members of Herman's Hermits (L-R) Barry Whitwam, Karl Green, Derek Leckenby and Peter Noone join EKU student newspaper reporter Buddy Anderson (far right) as guests at the Anderson home in Ashland, Kentucky during a break from the Dick Clark Caravan of Stars tour. Anderson is brother of Jon Anderson of Action Unlimited.

Dewey Pope at the Action Unlimited Reunion at Gravel Switch, Kentucky, 2003

Action Unlimited Reunion 2003

and holding it down, coughing a lot in the process. After a very short time, I started feeling very mellow and time seemed to really slow down. I went back on the stage for the second set and started playing. I noticed that all the guys were looking back at me, with Kent finally leaning over to me and saying, "Dewey, you're not just a beat behind, you're a song behind." The band had to quit so I could leave the stage, go outside, get some fresh air and walk around to get back to my normal self. I recovered pretty quickly, mainly because I hadn't smoked that much of the joint. For the record, to borrow from Tom Petty and the Heartbreakers, that was my last dance with Mary Jane. I never smoked marijuana again.

Also, while we were in Oxnard, Riley had set up an audition for us with Irene James, who was the owner/operator of a club in Palm Springs, California named I.J.'s. We actually took a day, traveled back down to Hollywood and did the audition at the Trip Club on the Sunset Strip in Hollywood. This was the club where we did our first audition to play at the Red Velvet several months back. As young and naïve as we were back then, we were now seasoned veterans, especially on the West Coast club circuit. And Cameo-Parkway would be releasing our record nationally soon.

Irene loved the band and booked us for the month of November at the club. It would be several weeks before November, so Riley booked us back at the Embers in Redwood City, California, and the Tiger a Go-Go in San Francisco. It was our second time for both places. It was good to get back to The Embers club, as we had made a lot of friends there from the first time and it was a fun club to play. The main thing that I remember about the second time in Frisco was that it was in early October and getting cooler. There always seemed to be a cool breeze somewhere, requiring a light jacket. It seemed to be warmer when we were there the first time in the spring. Also, we met a wide variety of people in the Tiger who stopped in for a drink between flights, giving us a lot of exposure that we didn't get in the other clubs. Riley informed us that our next booking would be in Ogden, Utah, which was a good distance away from San Francisco and farther inland than we had been since our Clark tour back in the winter. We were also still very excited about the October release of our record.

When we left San Francisco, it was great fall weather, cool but comfortable. It was jacket weather, and we did not anticipate running into cold weather anytime soon. By the time we crossed the border into Utah, we had to stop at a truck stop and run in to buy some warm clothing, as it was very cold, especially at night. I remember buying a set of long underwear, as the panel truck did not have a great heater and I was freezing. We had all gotten rid of our winter-type clothing since the past winter, as we had gotten spoiled by the warm California and Oregon weather throughout the spring and summer. I remember driving through Salt Lake City on our way to Ogden and how beautiful the area was, especially with all the mountains.

Ogden was the first place that I became somewhat homesick because it reminded me so much of Lexington. This was strange because I had enjoyed my time tremendously on the West Coast, never getting homesick, but there was something about Ogden that really got to me. Ogden's main street was very similar to Lexington's, which reminded me of the times when I was a lot younger, making the special "Saturday" trips to Lexington from Winchester on the train. Those were special trips because Lexington was the "big city," and it was a great adventure as a kid to get up on Saturday mornings, ride the train over, spend the day, and ride back in the afternoon. I think I was homesick for the entire two weeks we were there.

The club we worked at was really nice, and we discovered on our first night there that it was deer season, with all the males going to the mountains to hunt, leaving the wives to fend on their own. Needless to say, the entire audience of the club every night for the two weeks was female, but believe it or not, they behaved themselves and were a great audience to play for. The club had a BYOB policy, which was bring your own bottle, I guess because of the area being dry.

We stayed at a motel very close to the club, and in a letter that Dave wrote to his daughter years later he recalled the night in Ogden, Utah, when we spent until sun-up trying to break into my room while my roommate Ole Sam was, shall we say, sound asleep. I think that was the only time that I didn't room with Kent, and I returned to the room I shared with Sam to find the door locked. Whether Sam was "busy" or just passed out from drinking, Dave didn't know, and I don't remember.

We did take a day to go up to one of the ski areas and got a great view of the Wasatch Mountain range. There was no snow at that time on the slopes, but you could sense that it wouldn't be long until the place would be packed with skiers. Just about every vehicle that you saw in the area had a deer tied across the hood or top during that two-week period. Kent and I decided to go see the new movie *Fantastic Journey* at a drive-in theater. It was a great movie, but we had to keep the heater on in the hearse for the entire movie. We, again, got quite a few stares when we pulled into the drive-in in a hearse with "Action Unlimited" painted on the sides.

We also received the news from Riley the second week in Ogden that Cameo Parkway had pushed the release of our record back from October until December. Riley felt that it was because Cameo was putting a lot of promotion on one of its releases entitled "96 Tears" by Question Mark and the Mysterians. It was moving up the charts pretty fast, and they were diverting all their attention to it. We were devastated and really resented the push but could do nothing about it. We accepted it and looked forward to December, hoping that Cameo would do the same for us. We knew that our record had been produced by one of the best in the business, as well as being recorded in Columbia Studios, but felt that Cameo had let us down. But, at the same time, I remembered that we had been told several months earlier in Hollywood that the music business can change daily and to learn to ride with the flow.

Ironically, while we were at the club in Ogden, "96 Tears" was really getting popular. Chuk recalled:

"We kept getting requests for it ("96 Tears") anyway. For a new floor show, Osborn decided we'd all switch instruments on that song, where you (me) sang lead, he played drums, I played bass, Kent and Sam played horns, and we pulled it off, and the audience loved it."

We worked on that switch up for a couple of days, and it was a lot of fun doing it, but believe me, I was more comfortable on the drums than being an out front singer. We did it in Ogden but never performed it anywhere else after that. I think it had a lot to do with the feeling that Cameo had let us down on the October release, so it was a waiting game to see what they would do in December. We finished up the two weeks in Ogden and headed out to Palm Springs. One thing we knew for sure, it would be warmer there. It was also the only time that I hated to leave an area because I had grown so attached to Ogden. The Wasatch Mountain Range was one of the most beautiful areas that I had seen so far.

Chapter Fifteen

Palm Springs, California

On the trip down to Palm Springs from Ogden, we started having some mechanical troubles with both the hearse and panel truck. We had been really lucky through all the previous months but had also put a lot of pressure on both vehicles. For the first time, we started wondering how much longer they would last. We also still had the '53 Caddy. We forgot about the vehicles when we pulled into Palm Springs because it was fantastic. The weather was great, still pretty warm, but very comfortable.

Irene James met us when we pulled into the El Mirador Hotel, which was where I.J.'s, her club, was located. We were captivated by the hotel and its layout, which featured a bell tower, a golf course and an Olympic-size pool

As soon as we met Irene at the club, we were all taken again by how nice she was. We remembered her from the audition in L.A. and had really looked forward to playing in Palm Springs.

El Mirador Hotel in Palm Springs, California. Courtesy of PalmSpringsLife.com.

After meeting her at the hotel and unloading our equipment, she gave us an in-depth tour of Palm Springs. She took us to Frank Sinatra's home first, where she introduced us to George Jacobs, his personal valet. We then went on to Hoagy Carmichael's home. She was a close friend to Jacobs, Sinatra and Carmichael.

She then took us to where we would be staying, and this time it would not be a motel. Irene let the bands who performed at the club stay at a ranch house she owned in Palm Springs. The house was large, providing more than enough room for all of us to live in comfortably, with the rent for staying there being part of the agreed salary for playing at I.J.'s. I remember it saved us tremendously as we used the large kitchen and laundry facilities to cook our meals and do our laundry.

After the band house tour, she then took us throughout the rest of the city, showing us all the landmarks and attractions, returning later to the club to finish setting up all our equipment. The pool was right in front of the club, and it seemed always full night and day with guests staying at the hotel. This was going to be another month-long engagement, one that we liked, as I.J.'s was a great place to play.

The club itself was well laid out, with the stage on the front wall, seating to each side, and front, with the bar to the left of the stage at the main entrance. The seating consisted of both booths and tables. We had played some really nice clubs on the West Coast, but I.J.'s was definitely one of the nicest.

From the first night we started at the club, there seemed to be a steady stream of celebrities coming every night. I remember Pat Boone during the first week, and he had his trademark white buck shoes on. Lawrence Harvey, the English actor, came in quite often. I was a big fan from his portrayal of Col. William Travis in John Wayne's *The Alamo*. Bruce Johnston of The Beach Boys came in one night and sat in with us. We were all impressed with his playing and personality as well.

Irene knew all the celebrities and always made a point to personally introduce us. I remember one afternoon we were rehearsing, and she was on the phone with someone. I noticed she kept looking at me and finally asked me to come down to the phone, that someone wanted to talk to me. I was puzzled, as I had no idea who it could be. When I took the phone, I heard a voice say, "Hello, Dewey, this is James Garner." I was blown away, since he was the star of the *Maverick* television series and one of my favorite actors. He was very gracious and talked about his new movie *Grand Prix* that would be coming out soon. Irene knew him and had heard me mention that I was a big fan of his.

We actually saw several movie stars in Palm Springs, as it was a great getaway for them from the hustle and bustle of Hollywood. The band also took a day to ride the tram up to the summit of Palm Spring's Mount Jacinto. It was hot and dry when we got onto the tram with, to our amazement, several inches of snow at the top of the mountain. It was beautiful, and you had a great view for miles of everything around Palm Springs. I remember seeing a large body of water, asking what it was, and finding out that it was the Salton Sea. The Salton Sea has more salt water in concentration than the ocean but less than the Great Salt Lake in Utah. I also was close enough to San Diego to make a couple of trips down to continue my studies with Giovanni DeSimone.

Palm Springs was not just another gig for us, as it was like being on an extended vacation. Playing at the club was so enjoyable that it wasn't like work at all. There was a horse stable close to the band house, and I had a great love for horses and riding. I started going over every day and renting a horse to ride out on the desert trails. I eventually got to be good friends with the owner, Jim Chandler. Those desert rides were really great, especially with the beautiful desert scenery.

I remember watching the Macy's parade at the band house on Thanksgiving morning, with Irene later treating the band to a wonderful Thanksgiving dinner at the club. After the Thanksgiving holiday, we were anxiously awaiting the release of our record coming up the next month. Cameo had sent out some early DJ copies to Riley and Steve Clark for promotion, and she had enough to give all the band several copies each, but we could not give them out until the actual release.

Jon and Sam had a motorcycle wreck during the last week in Palm Springs, which caused extensive damage to Jon's left foot. Irene had a young man who took care of the maintenance at the house, and he had a Honda motorcycle that he kept there. He let all of us in the band use it if we needed to. We were having a going-away party at the house during the last weekend in Palm Springs, and Sam and Jon rode the bike to the liquor store several times. On the last trip back to the house, with Jon behind Sam on the bike, they had the accident. They pushed the bike back to the house, and Jon made it to the shower, where we all went to check on him. He was standing in the shower, in a pool of blood from his foot, and we immediately took him to the hospital.

They treated him, bandaged up the wound, and made a follow-up appointment for him. Jon recalled:

"After I had seen the doctor and gotten bandaged up, the orderly pushed me back out to the waiting room to get the follow-up appointment. When he left to do that, I glanced over and saw the exit sign, so I got up on my crutches and hobbled out, knowing I had to play that night. The hospital was close to the club, so I made it there and played on stage on the crutches. I didn't go back for the follow-up, which turned out later to be a mistake, as I developed a pretty serious infection."

The month in Palm Springs went by very quickly, and Riley informed us that we would be going back to Portland, Oregon, for another month-long engagement there. It was hard leaving Palm Springs, as we had gotten spoiled with the club, weather, and celebrity atmosphere, but we enjoyed Portland before and knew it would be fun to go back.

The band that followed us into I.J.'s was the Nooney Rickett Band. We had heard quite a bit about them, especially in Las Vegas, and got to hear them on their first night there before we left. They were great.

Also, the hearse and panel truck had finally broken down in Palm Springs during that month, due to wear and tear, which was inevitable because of all the pressure we had put on them. It would have been too expensive to repair them, so we had to make the decision to get rid of both. Getting rid of those two vehicles was like losing best friends, as we had been through so much with them. That left us with the Caddy and, ironically, it caught fire and burned up. Chuk recalled that incident:

"I remember that I had a girlfriend from Portland who was a dancer. Her name was Midge, and Gail McConkey got her a dancing gig in a club up in Ridgecrest, California. I wanted to go see her during our weekend break, so Sam and I left after the Saturday night closing. We had just filled the tank about 20 miles back, with another 20 to go to get to Ridgecrest. It was about 4 a.m. in the middle of the desert, when the left rear tire on the Cadillac blew out. I was driving, with Sam riding shotgun. I turned off the engine and Sam said, 'What should we do now?' I was looking in the side view mirror, and I saw light flickering at the back tire. I said, 'I think we'd better get out. The tire's on fire.' I remember that there was some kind of problem with the passenger door, so Sam was trying to crawl over me to get out. We dove into a ditch on the other side of the road and scrambled up the other side and over. When we looked back, we saw flames under the car, right where the gas tank was. Sam or I said something about getting down a ways from the car before it exploded, so we worked our way down the side and came back onto the road to watch. Shortly, we saw a bright flash and whoomp! We walked back to the car to see it totally engulfed in flames. When we got back to Palm Springs, Dave said in apparent exasperation, 'I guess I'll have to go up there to get the car.' I then presented him with a nine-inch string of glass with a pretty droplet of glass on the end. 'You don't understand,' I said. 'This is all that is left of the windshield.' Midge took pictures of the car, which had melted down to a slagheap about 12 inches high. The State of California sent us a bill for the pavement we burned up, and another for a telephone pole, which had the misfortune of being too close to the Caddy when it went. Now, here's the kicker. Turns out that Dave knew we had a bad left rear wheel bearing going out but didn't think we could afford to get it fixed. If we hadn't taken that trip, then next time we went on a lengthy drive (to our next gig), we would have had the U-Haul, with all of our equipment attached to it. We would have lost everything and maybe [our] lives, too."

We had to rent a car and U-Haul trailer to get our equipment up to Portland. I remember it was a long drive from southern California all the way up to Portland. The sway bar on the car hitch was not adjusted properly, and we thought we were going to lose the trailer a couple of times. We stopped in Shasta and had a new sway bar installed. I don't know if this was a sign of things to come, but things were really about to change for the band in the coming weeks.

Chapter Sixteen

Back to Portland

When we got to Portland in early December, it was cool but not uncomfortable. Christmas was coming on, and there were decorations everywhere. We stayed at the same motel that we had back in August, and everyone at the Town Mart club was glad to see us return. We looked forward to playing and spending the holidays there, as it was a great atmosphere, especially during the Christmas holidays.

The first week at the club went really well, with good crowds and great receptions to our floor shows. Jon was still having trouble with his foot from the bike accident, and I don't remember if he went in to have it checked there or not. Doug Crombie was back at the club almost every night, and he brought in a friend who was a teacher at one of the high schools in the area. He liked the band so well that he wanted us to come out and do a concert for the students. With the record coming out any day, we decided to do the concert, as it would be a great promotional event for the Portland area.

We did the concert in the gym of the high school in the afternoon with a full house of students. We didn't know if our style of music would go over with the students, but they loved it and gave us a fantastic reception with an autograph session afterwards.

The school newspaper featured a story about us. There were a lot of misspellings in the story with the "Louisville Sound" being misspelled as the "Lovesville" sound and Chuk's name spelled Frisko instead of Trisko. Dave's last name was spelled Asborn instead of Osborn. We didn't appear on the *Shindig!* television show but did do the "Shindig!" show for the U.S. Navy in Long Beach, California. We were scheduled to appear with Ronnie Dove but that later fell through and finally we had already had our recording session with Columbia (actually the story was written after we had been scheduled back into the studio in early January). Regardless, the article was well appreciated by the band, and we enjoyed their enthusiasm in having us perform for them.

Our record was released nationally in early December and, according to Riley, was selected as "Pick Hit of the Week" in several markets but over the next few weeks never made it into the top 100. We were really let down, naturally, but again were at the mercy of the record label and their timetable. We were puzzled, but at least glad that the record had done well in some of the markets. Riley assured us that was encouraging and to not give up hope. She later informed us that Cameo wanted to put us back in the studio and do another cut that would be more representative of the band. Evidently they felt, like we did, that the first record with the "psychedelic" effect was not truly who we were, and it wasn't. Riley and Steve Clark scheduled us back to Hollywood and Columbia Studios in January 1967.

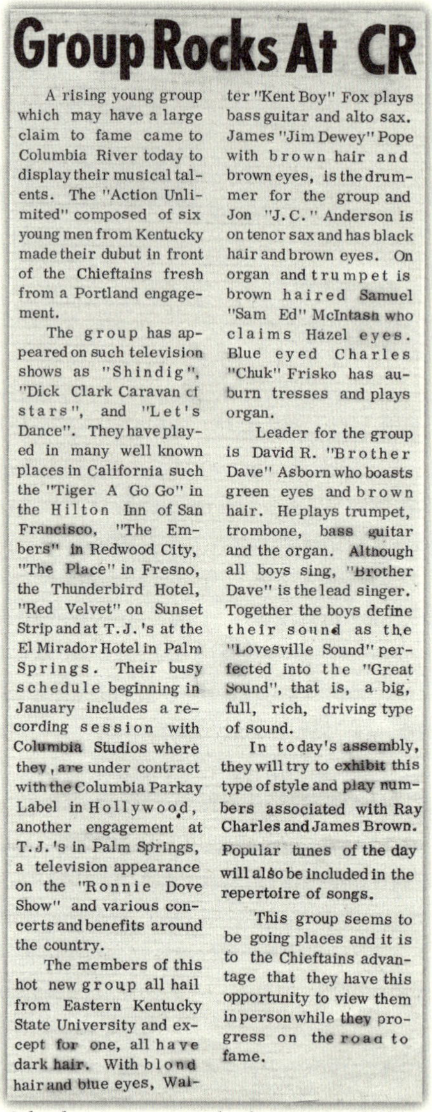

Group Rocks At CR

A rising young group which may have a large claim to fame came to Columbia River today to display their musical talents. The "Action Unlimited" composed of six young men from Kentucky made their dubut in front of the Chieftains fresh from a Portland engagement.

The group has appeared on such television shows as "Shindig", "Dick Clark Caravan cf stars", and "Let's Dance". They have played in many well known places in California such the "Tiger A Go Go" in the Hilton Inn of San Francisco, "The Embers" in Redwood City, "The Place" in Fresno, the Thunderbird Hotel, "Red Velvet" on Sunset Strip and at T. J.'s at the El Mirador Hotel in Palm Springs. Their busy schedule beginning in January includes a recording session with Columbia Studios where they, are under contract with the Columbia Parkay Label in Hollywood, another engagement at T. J.'s in Palm Springs, a television appearance on the "Ronnie Dove Show" and various concerts and benefits around the country.

The members of this hot new group all hail from Eastern Kentucky State University and except for one, all have dark hair. With blond hair and blue eyes, Walter "Kent Boy" Fox plays bass guitar and alto sax. James "Jim Dewey" Pope with brown hair and brown eyes, is the drummer for the group and Jon "J. C." Anderson is on tenor sax and has black hair and brown eyes. On organ and trumpet is brown haired Samuel "Sam Ed" McIntash who claims Hazel eyes. Blue eyed Charles "Chuk" Frisko has auburn tresses and plays organ.

Leader for the group is David R. "Brother Dave" Asborn who boasts green eyes and brown hair. He plays trumpet, trombone, bass guitar and the organ. Although all boys sing, "Brother Dave" is the lead singer. Together the boys define their sound as the "Lovesville Sound" perfected into the "Great Sound", that is, a big, full, rich, driving type of sound.

In today's assembly, they will try to exhibit this type of style and play numbers associated with Ray Charles and James Brown. Popular tunes of the day will also be included in the repertoire of songs.

This group seems to be going places and it is to the Chieftains advantage that they have this opportunity to view them in person while they progress on the road to fame.

School newspaper article about Action Unlimited appearance at their assembly

As I've mentioned before, something was about to happen that would have a great impact on the band. Everything was going well in Portland. The club crowds were great, and even though we didn't have the results we wanted with the first record, we were excited about going back into the studio.

We were all in Dave's room early into the second week when we heard the knock on the door. When we answered the door, it was two men in dark suits asking for Dave Osborn. Dave came forward to greet them, upon which they told him that he had to come with them to report to the draft board in Portland. I don't remember him even having time to grab his coat as they escorted him straight to their car. We followed them out, asking where the board was, to which they answered that we could follow if we wanted to. Of course, Riley and the rest of us followed them to the draft board location.

We were all puzzled, as we thought that Riley had taken care of Dave's draft situation from the last time we were in Portland. She mentioned that she had been in contact with the board but had not heard back and thought that all was okay. They were waiting for us to get back to Portland to serve him for the second time with a draft notice. That was not hard to figure out, as it was well advertised that we were back at the Town Mart Club.

After following the car to the draft board location, entering the building and asking about Dave, we were told that we couldn't see him as he would be going through testing, medical screenings and other things involved with being inducted into military service. We spent the entire day there waiting, hoping that he would not be accepted, as "induction into military service" sounded pretty serious to us.

They finally brought him out late that afternoon with orders for him to report back the next morning at 8 a.m. for induction into military service. We were shocked, and puzzled, that this could happen so quickly. Things were looking so good for the band, and this would definitely have an impact on everything that we had accomplished the past ten months. We knew the band couldn't go on without Dave. He was the leader, the lifeline and the one person who we all depended on. He was the "rock" of the band.

It was a very quiet ride back to the motel and a late night as we sat up discussing the situation. I think it was the first time that I had ever seen Dave at a loss of words. He was very quiet. We knew there was nothing we could do about it, no options available, as he was going to be inducted the next morning. It would, very possibly, be the last we would see of him for a long time. At one time during the session, we talked about disbanding and picking back up when Dave got out. There was also the reality of him going to Vietnam and whether or not he would make it back from there. It was the most serious and disheartening event that we had faced since we arrived in California. All we could do was take him in the next morning and say our goodbyes.

Again, it was a long night, and we didn't know what to expect the next morning. We took Dave in, reporting promptly at 8 a.m. He told us all not to worry, that everything would be okay. We didn't leave, as we had decided to stay until we found out his status. Finally, in the late afternoon, a representative came out and told us that Dave was being transferred to a hospital in the Portland area for further evaluation.

We don't know what happened that day that changed him from being inducted to being transferred to another facility, especially a hospital. It was then, and still is, a mystery as to what Dave did or didn't do to facilitate the transfer. We later found out that the hospital was actually a mental hospital and that he would be there for a while. Everything with the draft board personnel was very vague, as we were not told anything other than the transfer and further evaluation.

It was, for the second time, a long ride back to the motel, without Dave this time. We were glad that he was not inducted, but had no idea what awaited him in a mental facility and how we would do without him for the next few weeks at the club.

After arriving back at the motel, we had a meeting to try to sort out a plan of action for the immediate future of the band. We had to play that night and knew it would be really hard without him. We talked to Doug Crombie about sitting in temporarily for Dave and through him also found a trumpet player who could fill in. It was not only losing a key player in the band, but also a family member, as we were all so close.

The next day we found the hospital address, called and were told that we could not see him for a few days. We finally were able to visit him the following weekend and it was a strange experience. It was a hospital for the mentally ill, but Dave was fine, again telling us not to worry that all would be okay. He didn't talk about what happened at the draft board, and we didn't ask, as we could tell it was not something he wanted to discuss. On our first visit, the hospital staff knew that Dave was a musician and that we were in the band with him, so they asked if we could perform something for the patients. We complied and did an arrangement of one of our songs with Sam at the piano in the break room. The patients loved it, and we were quite the celebrities at every visit from then on.

I don't know what kind of treatment that Dave received at the hospital, as he didn't talk about that either. We did talk to a couple of his doctors but didn't learn much. It was noticeable on every visit that he seemed to be withdrawing within himself, and that was troubling as he had always been very outgoing. The main focus for us was to encourage him, stay positive and keep everything going until he was released.

Christmas was coming up, and we decided to take a few days off from the club and fly back home to visit our families. We had already talked about this earlier in the year. We knew Dave was going to be in the hospital through the holidays, and he encouraged the vacation, as he felt that it would be good for us. As serious as his situation was, he was still concerned about the welfare of the band. We felt really bad for him having to spend the holidays there, but we knew, as did he, that there was nothing that could be done about it. He was there until they decided to let him out. Also, taking the time off would help us with getting through the nights at the club without Dave. Even with the replacements, as good as they were, we were not the same without him.

The club found a replacement band for us, and we flew out a few days before Christmas, planning to return on New Year's Day. We visited the hospital the night before we left, taking him Christmas gifts from the band. It was very emotional, knowing that we were coming back home without Dave. He handled it better than us, again constantly reassuring us that he was fine and not to worry. I don't think anyone of us enjoyed the flight back, but I knew that being home would help take our minds off it.

Chapter Seventeen

Christmas in Kentucky, Then Back to Portland

The one thing that did help somewhat to take our minds off Dave was the Christmas season coming on. I remember Portland was beautiful during the Christmas season, especially the large mall that we visited several times. I don't remember the name of the mall, but it was huge, with Christmas decorations everywhere.

Before we left, Kent's Christmas gift to me was a new snare drum stand. My old stand had just about fallen apart, and a new one was well needed. My gift to him was a new strap for his bass and a St. Christopher Medal with "Action Unlimited" engraved on it. We drew names for Christmas gifts and had even decorated our motel rooms to get into the Christmas spirit.

On the flight home, Jon's foot (the injury from the motorcycle accident in Palm Springs) was still giving him problems. We thought he had seen a doctor in Portland, but evidently he hadn't. He must have endured the pain tremendously during the past weeks on stage, as we never noticed any difference in his stage antics. He didn't realize that the wound had become infected, finding out when he got home that it had seriously worsened. The stewardess on the plane helped him to change to an aisle seat so he could straighten his leg out during the flight.

We flew from Portland to Chicago and then onto Lexington. When we arrived in Lexington, Chuk's family, Kent's family, Jon's family, Sam's family and several of our friends were all waiting to greet us. It was a great reunion, and we were happy to be home. There was a lot of talk at the airport about our long hair, as most of us had shorter haircuts when we left Kentucky months before. We got a lot of stares from the people in the airport, as I'm sure they were wondering who we were from all the commotion from our families and friends.

I rode from the airport back to Winchester with Kent and his Mom and Dad, as my family was unable to be there. My mother was sick, had been in the hospital, and my father was taking care of her. When I arrived home, my brother and his family from Texas were there, also helping Dad to take of my mother. It was another great reunion, as I hadn't seen my brother in a few years. My parents were elated to see me, and we sat up late talking about all that had happened, especially with the current record (it was still getting played in several markets) and the new one we were going to record in January. It was wonderful to be home.

The next couple of days were hectic, as Kent and I spent a lot of time visiting friends and catching everybody up on the band and all that we had accomplished the past year. We visited the high school that we graduated from and were treated like celebrities, taking pictures and signing autographs. Kent and I visited the band practice of a local band named The Utmost. We both had friends in the band and had a great time visiting with them. They were very popular throughout Kentucky, and were really curious about California and the band scene on the West Coast. I remember there was a Christmas party held in our honor by some of our close friends.

Kent and I visited Speck's and a couple of clubs in Lexington, and it was uncanny as I remembered how much Ogden, Utah, reminded me of Lexington and vice versa. Everyone was glad to see us and very interested in how the band was doing. We were on the go constantly, which made the time go by fast. Christmas actually came and went pretty quickly it seemed. We did get some rest time the week after, and I remember wondering about Dave and how Christmas had been for him in the hospital in Portland.

My mother's health improved tremendously during the time I was in, even to the point during the second week that she was up fixing her usual good dinners. She was a great cook, and I did miss her home cooking while I was gone. My dad fixed me breakfast every morning, as he was always up early and could cook up a great batch of eggs and bacon. I went to a New Year's Eve party in 1967, wondering what the new year would bring for the band. We flew out on New Year's Day, as we had to play the next night. It was great to be home for the holidays, but it went fast. We all knew that we had to get back to Portland, the band and Dave.

On the flight back to Kentucky we flew into Lexington, but on the way back to the West Coast, we flew out of Louisville due to connections that were needed for Portland. When we all met up at the airport, everyone had great stories to tell about their visits back home. Jon had seen a doctor in Ashland, who treated the infection on his foot, doing a remarkable job as it was almost completely healed. Jon kept a close watch on it from that point on and had no more problems with it.

I was on a window seat flying back, and as we were approaching the Portland area, I looked out to see a full moon shining on the complete cloud cover below us, creating a beautiful surreal silver effect. I then saw Mount Hood rising out of the clouds with its snow-covered peak looking majestic in the moonlight. It was very calming, and one of the most beautiful sights that I had ever seen.

I couldn't help but wonder what was in store for us with this new year coming on and if it would be anything like the year before. We had accomplished a lot, but still had a long way to go. Would this new record put us over the top? All we could do was stay positive, hope for the best, and get Dave back into the band.

When we arrived back in Portland, we visited Dave as soon as we were settled in. He was fine, with us giving him all the news from back home, especially on his family and year-old twin daughters, which really pleased him. We spent a lot of time with him on that first visit back, and by the time we left, he was his old self again.

At the club, Doug Crombie was sitting in with us indefinitely and doing a great job. It was very hard for him to step in and cover for Dave. We were very impressed with him, his personality and his playing. We were also still using the trumpet player we used before Christmas.

During the next couple of weeks, we visited Dave every chance we could, anxiously awaiting a decision on when he could be released. Riley had persuaded Steve Clark to hold off on the next recording session until Dave was out of the hospital. She had also booked us back into I.J.'s in Palm Springs after the session for a six-week stint.

Finally, in mid-January, Riley received a call to come to the hospital to pick Dave up. He was being released with a 4F classification for the draft. They explained that the 4F classification meant that he was totally unqualified for military service, so he didn't have to worry about being called up again. Again, what happened at the hospital we didn't know, only that he was evaluated and released after almost a month-and-a-half.

We all went together to pick him up and took him out for a celebration dinner. He seemed to be fine, and we were really looking forward to getting him back on stage into the environment that he did so well in. He went right back on stage and picked up where he left off.

There were times when he seemed to lose some of the important leadership skills he had before, but Riley always took over to help him out. Jon also took over the stage leadership as he was always Dave's right hand man. There was a change in Dave. He was not the same at times, but we could tell he was trying. It was hard to imagine what he had gone through during his stay at the hospital and what they had done to him in the evaluation process. He never talked about it, and we never asked.

On our first night off from the club after he came back, the band decided to take an overnight trip up to the lodge on Mount Hood. It was a great way to get away and enjoy some downtime with each other. It was a winter wonderland, snow everywhere, with great meals and service at the lodge. It helped us to get our focus back on the new year coming and the new recording session coming up. Dave was back, and we were back on track.

Chapter Eighteen

Back to Hollywood, Our Second Recording Session, and Palm Springs Again

We left Portland and headed back to Hollywood for the recording session at Columbia Studios. It was good to be back in California, as we had a rough few weeks in Portland. We loved playing there but were glad to leave Dave's hospital situation behind us. The trip home for Christmas was revitalizing in many ways, but we still felt bad for him having to miss that. We had no idea when we arrived in Portland, a month-and-a-half before, of what was in store for us.

It was hard to leave Doug Crombie behind. He had been a huge lift for us, filling in for Dave, but we knew we would see him again, probably on another return trip back to play at the Town Mart in the future. It was also hard to accept that our record had not done better than we anticipated, but the good thing was knowing we were on our way to the studio to cut another one.

Upon arriving in Hollywood, we found out that we would be staying at a major hotel in Hollywood with all expenses paid for a week while we worked on the new record. It would be the same process as before, with the music tracks already cut. This time we had a song that had been written by someone else. Steve Clark Production Agency was also again producing. The music was more of who we were, with horns and a strong R&B feel. We spent the days working on the vocal tracks and nights enjoying the nightlife of Hollywood. I remember everyone being pleased with the overall feel of this new one. The name of the "A" side would be "Take My Hand." The plan was to spend the week getting the "A" side completed and then come back at a later date to do the "B" side. Sam again sang the lead, with the band providing the backup harmony vocals as before on the first record. Riley told us that Cameo would have a summer release date for this one and get behind it all the way.

We finished the recording session in Hollywood and headed to Palm Springs for a two-month stint. We were excited about the record and what the new year would bring for us. It was also great to be back in Palm Springs, as it we felt it was a great place for us to get back on track.

As before, I.J.'s club was continually loaded with celebrities every night, which really encouraged us. Lawrence Harvey was still coming into the club, as well as Hoagy Carmichael and Dennis Wilson, the Beach Boys' drummer. I remember looking out one night from the drums as we were playing and seeing Gary Collins (the star of the television Western *The Iron Horse*) and his wife, Mary Ann Mobley (the former Miss America) on the dance floor. It seemed like almost every night Irene was introducing us to some celebrity in the audience.

Dave was doing well, although there were times when Riley seemed to be making all the band decisions whereas before they worked closely together. It was noticeable that he did withdraw into himself at times, leaving Riley and Jon to keep things going. He definitely was not the same Dave as before the hospital stay, but we all felt this would pass. The main focus now was to concentrate on our new record and to get ready for whatever lay ahead for us.

As mentioned before, there was talk of appearing with Ronnie Dove after the first of the year, but that fell through. Riley also was working on having us going on the road with Gene Pitney, but that also fell through. We had a lot of disappointments but knew that Riley was constantly working on keeping us busy and in the forefront as much as possible.

I also managed to get back down to San Diego again for another drum lesson with Giovanni DiSimone. I was really starting to grow as a drummer, experimenting more with things that I had never used before, including using "ghost notes" on the snare and incorporating more rudiments into my playing. All of these things came from studying with Giovanni as he really helped me to think and play more outside the box.

After a couple of weeks at the club, a rodeo came to town, complete with a "celebrity parade of stars," so we all decided to spend a Saturday afternoon at the rodeo. We went to the parade first, which was held on the main thoroughfare of Palm Springs. The parade and rodeo had several stars of television Westerns including Richard Long and Lee Majors of *The Big Valley*; Slim Pickens, Andrew Prine and Glenn Corbett of *The Road West*; and Johnny Crawford of *The Rifleman*. We actually saw Slim Pickens when he arrived at the El Mirador Hotel where he stayed for the weekend but didn't get to meet him.

During one part of the parade, Lee Majors rode by on his horse, and Dave and Jon yelled out his "real name," upon which he turned around to see us with a look of surprise. Dave and Jon remembered him from Eastern Kentucky University, as that was where he went to college, knowing him by his real name. They both yelled, "We're from EKU and Kentucky," at which he smiled and responded, telling us to meet him at his hotel after the parade. After the parade, we went to the hotel but were told that he had been held up and would see us later. We went on to the rodeo, seeing all the stars make appearances at various times, with Johnny Crawford actually participating in the rodeo itself.

I was able to meet Slim Pickens as he came up and sat pretty close to us. I mentioned the movie *Flim-Flam Man*, which had parts that were filmed in Winchester, Kentucky, telling him that was where I was from. He was extremely nice and remembered Winchester. I also told him that I was playing in the band at I.J.'s (which was part of the El Mirador Hotel where he was staying), asking him to come hear us later that night. He said he would.

About midway through the afternoon, I went to the concession stand, and as I was standing there I looked around and Lee Majors was standing right beside me. I introduced myself, told him I was from Kentucky, playing at I.J.'s in Palm Springs with a band that had its origins from EKU. He remembered us from the parade, was very interested in the band because of EKU, and said he would come to the club later to hear us.

On the way back to the stands, I saw Andrew Prine and Glenn Corbett and invited them to the club later, with them saying they would be there as well. It was a fun afternoon and great experience seeing and meeting many of the stars who I had watched on television from a young age.

All the stars from the rodeo did show up at the club and had a great time. Lee Majors sat at our table, staying most of the night. The band had a great time talking with him about Kentucky and EKU. He was very humble and very complimentary of the band.

Chapter Nineteen

Chuk Leaves AU, Followed by Jon

The next few weeks at I.J.'s were typical. The band was playing great, although Riley was still taking over more for Dave. We didn't hear much from her or Steve Clark during that time about what was happening with our record and future with Cameo-Parkway records. For the first time, I was starting to see some discontent in the band. Jon recalled:

"Problem was that we had endured a string of setbacks and didn't make the trip to California to simply play clubs. We went west to score big. Finally, after months of conditioning and preparation, we were told to be in the producer's office ... Without an ounce of doubt, in any of our minds, we were only a signature on a contract away from cracking the big time. When the six of us arrived, we were told by the receptionist that Steve was running late… He never showed up… We looked at each other and simply walked out of the office and down the street without saying a word… We needed him, but he didn't need us. He had other talent waiting in the wings. We never heard from Steve again."

The setback with the first record, Dave's hospital stay in Portland, and the sudden lack of communication and interest from our production agency and record company definitely helped to create doubt in the band. Whereas before, in the earlier months, we were in constant contact with all of them, now we seemed to be in the dark about the band's future.

Finally, the inevitable happened. Chuk decided to leave the band and go back to Kentucky. I think he realized that the band was on the downhill slide and now was the time to go. It was heart-breaking news, and we all didn't want to accept it, but we had to. Chuk recalled:

"I was the first to leave. The follow-up to the second record never happened, probably because of Dave's draft issues, and his being put into the Oregon Hospital. After that, Dave never hit the high notes on his horn the same again and just seemed to stop trying."

We had been through so much with Chuk the past year. He wrote both songs on the first record. He was also the only one who had a separate contract as a writer, a publishing agreement with the production agency and record company. So, losing those connections did not help the band as well. He was a great showman on stage, along with being a tremendous lead guitar player, and was an original member of the Action Unlimited lineup from the spring of '65. We gave him a good send-off on his last night, with all of us accompanying him to the airport the next day. It was a huge loss, but we had to deal with it and move on.

Finding someone with the ability to play, sing and write would be hard. We auditioned a few guitar players in Palm Springs, not finding anyone we liked. We called Doug Crombie from Portland and asked him to come down. We knew he could play, especially with him knowing the arrangements from his time with us in Portland while Dave was in the hospital. He came down and auditioned, and we hired him on the spot.

We knew that we had lost one-sixth of the chemistry that the band had been built on for the last year and longer, counting the summer in Cincinnati. We continued on at I.J.'s, with Doug doing a great job, and actually got our spirits back up somewhat but had no idea that we were in for another setback.

Within a few weeks after Chuk left, Jon let us know that he was leaving. He told us that he was tired of making just enough for expenses and was becoming more and more disenchanted with the band not making it after all the time and work that we had invested. He was especially discontented with the current sudden lack of interest and commitment from both the production agency and record company. Jon recalled:

"Disenchantment was starting to set in and things started to change. I was the second member to leave the band. With the direction the band was starting to go in, my brother had a job lined up for me in Cincinnati that paid really good money and I just couldn't turn it down."

This would create another loss of important chemistry in the band and would eventually turn out to be catastrophic for the life of the band. We had to accept his departure and again started looking for a replacement. There was never a problem in finding musicians in the southern California area, as it was full of them. After trying out several musicians, we decided on hiring a saxophone player by the name of Hank Watkins. He had just come off the road with a major band and was looking for a new gig. He was a great musician, but it would be impossible to replace the chemistry that Jon had created. Jon was our number one showman on stage, our second in command, and an original all the way back to the very beginnings of The Maroons on EKU's campus and Action Unlimited during the summer of 1965.

We gave him a great sendoff by going with him up to Las Vegas on our night off (the night after his last night). Jon had bought Kent's car and was going to drive it back to Cincinnati. Dave, Sam and I drove up with him, spent the night partying and flew back to Palm Springs the next day. We were all broke the next morning, and had to wire Riley to send us money to pay for the flight back to Palm Springs. Jon drove on from Las Vegas back to Cincinnati.

With Chuk and now Jon gone, we had lost one third of the original chemistry that was very vital to the band, even though we had replaced both with great musicians. We also had more devastating news the last week in Palm Springs from Riley. She informed us that Cameo-Parkway had decided to drop us due to the major personnel changes in the band. Again, as mentioned before, Steve Clark Productions had dropped us as well, probably for the same reasons. Regardless of Riley's ability to make great things happen, it was starting to look like the dream was coming to an end.

Chapter Twenty

Kent, Then I Leave the Band

Riley booked us back in Oxnard, California, at the Carousel Club, after we finished up in Palm Springs. We had a great rapport with audiences there before, and I think she, as well as we, hoped that would help to revitalize the band, especially after the losses we had just gone through. Doug and Hank proved to be good choices, both musically and personality-wise. We were performing well again. Kent and I rented a trailer close to the club instead of staying at the motel. There was also a riding stable close by, and we spent a lot of our days riding the countryside around Oxnard on horseback.

We were hearing a lot about the Vietnam War during this time, especially on television. It seemed like every night we met someone at the club who had just returned. Some had stories to tell, and many of them never talked about it, only that they had been there and were glad to be home. When we would take our breaks, the house PA would play the current hits, and I remember hearing "California Dreaming" (by The Mamas and the Papas) several times a night. To this day, when I hear that song I think about the band, the Vietnam vets and their stories. I didn't realize until a few years later, when I went into the military, the scope of the Vietnam War and impact it had on America.

One night while we were playing at the Carousel, James Brown was playing a concert down the street from us in an open parking lot. We would go down on our breaks and listen to him and his band. That's when I got my first dose of Clyde Stubblefield and John (Jabo) Starks, the two drummers in the band. Their grooves were inspirational to me, especially the snare, kick drum and hit-hat patterns. I think, to this day, the impact from those grooves were very influential to all the drummers who came up during that time. It showed the importance of being a team member, supporting the band, and concentrating on the groove.

I was also starting to notice a change in Kent's enthusiasm and optimism toward the group, as well as mine. It was hard to be optimistic with all that had happened. We knew that unless Riley came up with some kind of miracle soon, the band was definitely in trouble. Even though we were playing well, the loss of our production agency and record label put us back to square one. I began to wonder who would be leaving next.

Just before we finished up the gig at the Carousel Club in Oxnard, Kent announced that he was leaving the group. This was devastating to me, but not shocking, as I knew he wasn't happy and wanted to pursue a solo career on his own. We had talked about leaving together, but I still wasn't sure what I wanted to do.

Riley called a meeting between her, Dave and me to discuss my plans for the band, as she knew Kent was definitely leaving with no chance of changing his mind. I told her that I was still undecided at the time. She talked me into staying with the group for a while longer, trying to keep at least three of the original members together that came out in February of '66. I remember Riley doing all the talking, with Dave being there but not saying much at all. I could see the hurt in his eyes from already losing Chuk, Jon and now Kent.

We finished the last week and gave Kent a good send-off. He was going back to Palm Springs to start a band of his own. It was really hard losing Chuk and Jon, but this one really affected me the most because of the relationship Kent and I had developed; we were best friends. We had started out together in The Monzzas just a few years earlier, not having any idea that we would take the musical journey that we had in Action Unlimited.

Kent and I had always had the ability to sync up together well. He was very conscious of my kick drum, and I was the same for his bass patterns, which provided a solid foundation for the band. He and I even came up with the idea of tuning my drums to his bass strings. We had a great rapport together and trusted each other's playing. He was only the second bass player that I had worked with since starting out with Paul Wasson in The Monzzas. I knew the band would really be different without him, especially for me, but I had decided to give it a try.

We again went through the auditions for a bass player. We replaced Kent with a bass player named Wayne Evans. He was a fine player and singer, with a pleasing personality. So, now we were down to three of the original six from Kentucky: Dave, Sam and me. We went back to L.A. and took a couple of weeks off to work Wayne in and plan the band's future.

Riley surprised us with a proposal we didn't expect. She had met a club owner from Atlanta, Georgia, who wanted us to come there and play for an extended engagement. I remember Doug and myself were not that crazy about going all the way to Atlanta, especially if it didn't have any possibilities of furthering our goals of getting on another record label. If we were going to settle into becoming a club band, it made more sense to stay on the West Coast circuit where we were at least well known. I didn't want to travel all the way back across the country to play in Atlanta. It was at that time that I knew the journey was over. It was time for me to leave.

Riley had already set up a double audition for us at the Ice House, one of the most popular clubs in the L.A. area, for both the Atlanta Club owner and the Ice House itself for a possible gig there. I gave my notice just before the audition. I told her I would stay until they found another drummer. We had rented a house in Long Beach during the time off to work in Wayne, and I knew it would also give them time to work in another drummer. Wayne knew a drummer and called him to come in for an audition. His name was Tony, and like Hank, he had just come off the road and was looking for another band to play in. We auditioned and hired him without trying out any others, as he was very good and seemed to fit in right away.

The band was now down to two original Kentucky members, Dave and Sam. It was definitely not the same band as a year-and-a-half earlier, but they had decided to keep it going regardless. We did the audition and were hired by both. The band would start at the Ice House the following week and go to Atlanta in July.

After the audition, we went back to the house and the guys had a going-away party for me. It was really strange not having Chuk, Jon and Kent there, but so much had changed, and I was very appreciative for the party. It was very emotional for me, as it would be hard to leave them. I wasn't leaving for any personal reasons, especially with Dave, Sam and Riley; I just knew it was time to go.

I had decided to go back to Kentucky. Wayne and Doug took me to the bus station early the next morning, as I had become very good friends with both, and they wanted to see me off. I sent my drums all the way back separately and bought a ticket to Phoenix, Arizona, so I could stop and see my brother on the way home. I didn't have enough money to fly home, with the bus trip being more affordable. I had said all my goodbyes the night before, so we left without waking everybody up. I came out to California in a hearse and panel truck and went back to Kentucky on a bus.

From the very beginning in 1956 at the Hickman Street Elementary School gym to a musical journey starting with my first drum set in July 1963 and ending almost a month to the day, four years later in June 1967, I went from a being a kid with a dream to playing with a band that touched on the very brink of national success, Action Unlimited.

"AU" is the symbol for gold, defined as "something valued as the finest of its kind." Action Unlimited was composed of six young men from Kentucky who took a musical journey, creating a legacy of "gold" for years to come.

Epilogue

The band's journey was over. We had accomplished so much for a band that just picked up and traveled across the country to California with no guarantees. The band had performed on Dick Clark tours and played at The Thunderbird Hotel in Las Vegas. We were accepted into a major Hollywood production agency, working with Steve Clark, Curt Boettcher, The Association and Tommy Roe. We made it onto a major record label and released a national record, "My Heart Cries Out." We shared the stage with many national acts, including Herman's Hermits, Little Anthony & The Imperials, Bobby Vee, Brian Hyland, Billy Joe Royal, Sir Douglas Quintet, Tom Jones, Peter and Gordon, The Turtles, The Beach Boys, Roy Head, The Coasters, George McCannon III, Billy Preston, The Newbeats, Jimmy O'Neill, Gary Edwards, The Results and several others. And we became a well-known band on the West Coast club circuit.

Even though Dave changed a lot after Portland, I still respected him and admired his talent. I knew that the band was his number one priority and that whatever he did to bring on the hospital stay, he felt it was for the good of the band. I had great admiration and respect for all the other guys in the band as well: Kent, Jon, Sam and Chuk. It was a great honor and privilege for me to take the musical journey with these fine musicians. I learned a lot from each of them and still consider them as brothers to this day. I also respected Riley and was very grateful for the journey that she provided for us because, when it came down to it, Riley was the catalyst for the whole experience. She believed in the band from the very beginning, taking it from being a local Kentucky group to a working prominent West Coast band with a major recording contract.

With four of the original Kentucky members gone, Action Unlimited continued on, going to Atlanta and eventually coming back to

Portland, where the group finally broke up in the fall of 1967. Riley's magic had finally worn off, although it was phenomenal what she had accomplished in such a short time for the band. I was never in contact with her after I left the band, but I heard that she had passed on a few years later. I still think of her often, and I know that no other manager could have worked as hard for the band as she did. Jon said it best: "As long as she had a pulse, she was promoting the band." She brought us very close, but it just wasn't meant to be.

Action Unlimited, 1967

Afterword

Dave Osborn

Dave Osborn, 1966

After the breakup of the band in Portland, Dave stayed on the West Coast and traveled with several other bands over the years, including USO tours overseas. All of us in the band lost contact with Dave from the late '60s on, not knowing where he was or what he was doing. We did find out many years later that he eventually came back to Louisville, settling into his childhood home, and never reunited with Jeanne.

His twin daughters, Dawn and Dava, grew up and carried on his musical tradition by performing as a duo throughout Kentucky. Dava died in 2000 from a congenital heart condition, and Dawn still performs in the central Kentucky area. The twins eventually did make contact with him, and in one of his letters to Dava, Dave mentions: "You and Dawn had expressed your concerns about the unpredictability of the music business, and I'm glad to hear that you know it involves a bit more than just stepping up to the mic and singing a pretty song." This was probably a nod to what he and AU had gone through years before.

In an incredible coincidence, I ended up working with Dawn during the '80s when she came to work at the same company that I worked for in the same department. I was a graphic artist and she was hired into the Print Shop. My boss wanted me to talk to her as we would be working closely together. When I first talked to Dawn, she mentioned that her dad was a musician. I then mentioned that I was a musician also. She went on to say that her father had gone to California with a band in the '60s. I then told her that I had gone to California with a band in the '60s as well. The conversation went on, and I asked her who her father was, and she said Dave Osborn. You can imagine my jaw dropping when I heard that. I then told her that I had gone to California with him and the same band and knew her father well, even being at the hospital to see her and her twin a few days after she was born.

Dave had heard that Dawn and I were working together years later in Danville, and he went on to write: "Dewey was always one of my favorites in that group (Action Unlimited); always laughing and full of devilment. Of all the guys, Dewey was in a class by himself. I've thought of him often, give him my best."

Dave's ex-wife Jeanne called me in 2012 to let me know that he was in Louisville, had a stroke, and was in serious condition. They (Jeanne and Dawn) had him moved from the hospital there to an assisted living home close to them. When they went through his personal belong-

Dave Osborn with wife Jeanne Lane, 2015

ings at his house, Dawn found military type identification cards that were probably used on USO tours. She mentioned that, in her communication with him, he had talked about traveling overseas several times with various bands as a trumpet player. I knew Dave was very patriotic from the very beginning, and maybe this was his way of serving after not being taken in Portland back in '66.

He recovered from the stroke but does not have the ability to communicate verbally. I was able to visit him in October 2016, and he is doing well. The wall in his room beside his bed is covered with several pictures of The Maroons and Action Unlimited. As of 2016, Jeanne is still operating Penn's Grocery in Gravel Switch, and Dave is 73 years old.

Jon Anderson

Jon went back to Cincinnati for a job in drafting, which was part of his industrial arts major at Eastern Kentucky University. He was a draftsman during the day, playing saxophone at a local club at night. Jon returned to California and played in a group named Union Square, which was based out of San Francisco. The group stayed together for a year before disbanding, upon which he returned home and went back into drafting.

Jon Anderson, 1966

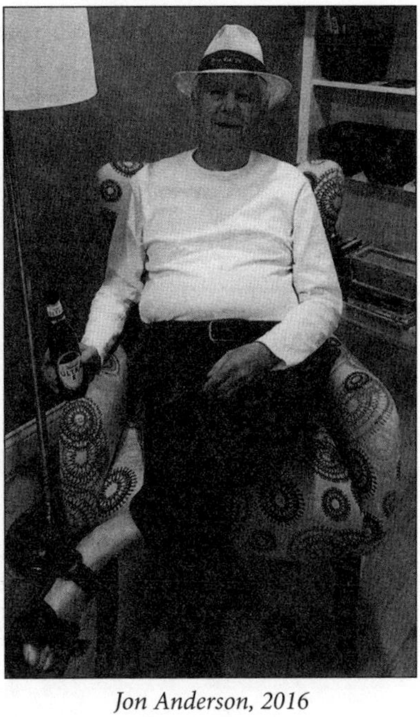

Jon Anderson, 2016

I did get a chance to visit Jon in 1969, spending the weekend with him when he lived in the Mount Adams area of Cincinnati. In 1974, he answered an ad for a disc jockey position at a new discotheque and got the job, saying it was way more fun than drafting, prompting him to again to change his career. This led to him getting his own equipment and becoming a party deejay, lasting for the next twelve years. In 1986, he left the deejay profession and returned to drafting, until his retirement in 2008.

Jon married his wife Jan in 1975, and they have two children, in addition to his son from an earlier marriage. I have seen him a few times over the years, and he is still the same Jon, always with a smile and very entertaining. Jon's children have rewarding careers, and he and Jan are currently enjoying their retirement. Jon was 73 years old in 2016.

Sam McIntosh

Sam stayed on the West Coast with Dave until the group broke up. He traveled all over the West Coast club and hotel circuit, performing with bands throughout the '70s and '80s. He never returned to live in Kentucky, but was in and out of the state several times. He married Melissa and eventually settled in Fort Walton Beach, Florida. Sam has played in the Fort Walton Beach area for many years and has a landscaping business there. I have communicated with him several times up until 2012.

Sam McIntosh, 1966

Sam McIntosh, 2016

From then until this year, I and other members of AU could not get in touch with him, and we all were very worried about him. I found out recently that the reason we had not heard from him was because he was involved in an automobile accident in 2012, suffering very severe injuries. He is unable to walk from having neuropathy in both legs, is blind in one eye, has severe hearing loss and is on oxygen daily. His wife Melissa takes care of him in their home in Fort Walton Beach. Sam was 72 years old in 2016 and was very excited about the book.

Chuk Trisko

Chuk returned to Lexington, Kentucky, after leaving the band and finished his last year of high school. He left during his senior year of high school to go west with the band, still needing one half credit to graduate. Chuk's high school principal kept his original diploma back for him, in case he did return to finish, presenting him with that diploma when he graduated in 1967. He mentioned that when he returned to Lexington and school, all the bands around thought of him as a celebrity because he had gone to California, with some even asking him to come hear them play to give his opinion.

Chuk Trisko, 1966

He stayed in Lexington through the summer, returning to Portland, Oregon in the early fall of '67, just as AU was breaking up. He formed a club band using some former AU members and toured briefly until he received his draft notice in the fall of '67. Rather than be drafted, he enlisted in the Army Security Agency (ASA). He ultimately didn't go into the ASA but did get assignments to Thailand and Germany, where he played in a Special Services band made up of his army friends, winning the 6th Army Entertainment contest in 1971. Chuk and I were actually in Europe at the same time. He was serving in Germany and I was serving in Belgium. We didn't get to see each other but did talk on the phone.

Chuk Trisko, 2015

Chuk returned to California after being discharged, forming the groups Peter Moon and Mostly Jeff in Sacramento while working at the Sacramento Army Depot. After his first marriage ended in 1972, he met Susan Fraley in 1974, marrying her in 1975. They have a son, David, who was born in 1976. Both Chuk and Susan had daughters, Summer and Robin, from previous relationships.

When the Depot was shut down, he relocated to Port Townsend, Washington, working in real estate until the crash in 2009, after which he drove a commercial tractor-trailer for Schneider National for about a year-and-a-half, working the eleven western states, especially the I-5 corridor. He went on to continue his education, going to Peninsula College in Port Angeles, Washington, earning his AA degree, and now works as a medical assistant in Port Townsend, Washington. Chuk was 68 years old in 2016.

Kent Fox

Kent returned to Palm Springs after he left the group and started his solo career. He formed a group called Revolver and spent a few years playing on the West Coast and as far east as Phoenix, Arizona. He eventually left that group and performed as a single act doing private parties and clubs in the southern California area, including performing at Frank Sinatra's home.

Kent married Irene James, who was the owner of I.J.'s nightclub, in 1967. They had a son, Peter Kevin Fox, in 1968. MCA Records signed him in 1973, releasing his first record as a solo artist, "New York Calling Miami." The record went to number one in some major markets and to number 75 on the Billboard Hot 100. He also wrote two songs that Tennessee Ernie Ford recorded on his album, "It's Ford" on Capitol Records. Kent went on to found his own recording label, Mercantile Records, releasing several singles from 1975 to 1980, including "Ben

Kent Fox, 1966

Kent Fox, 2016

Franklin Said It" (which was co-written by Jack Fascinato, Tennessee Ernie Ford's arranger), "Midnight In The Morning," "Married To The Girl I Love" and "The Eight They Left Behind" (a tribute to the soldiers killed in the rescue attempt during the Iranian hostage crisis). Kent and Irene divorced in 1983, after which he left Palm Springs in 1986, moving to Nashville, Tennessee, to pursue his music career there.

He met and married Gloria Gill in 1992. Gloria is also a performer and has written several children's books. They've performed together since then, doing a combination of puppet shows, music, and teaching creative writing. Their shows, performed at fairs, festivals, schools and churches, were well received up and down the East Coast and in the South, as well. He and Gloria are now retired and living in Mount Juliet, Tennessee. We are still close friends and stay in touch on a regular basis. Kent was 69 years old in 2016.

Dewey Pope

I returned to Kentucky in 1967 and played drums locally for the next two years. I joined the Army in 1969 and served stateside and overseas. I served as an Entertainment Specialist in the Army's Special Services Branch at SHAPE Headquarters in Brussels, Belgium, both as a musician and army illustrator.

Dewey Pope, 1966

Dewey Pope, 2016

After my stint in the army, I returned to Kentucky and enrolled at Eastern Kentucky University, eventually obtaining a degree in art in 1979. I went on to work as an illustrator, graphic illustrator and visual arts specialist for the next several years in Kentucky. I went back into the military, joining the Army Reserves in 1981, and moved onto the Kentucky Army National Guard in 1985.

I served as a graphic illustrator, photojournalist and visual information manager for the next 24 years while in the Guard. I directed and edited a documentary in 2003, *The History of the Kentucky National Guard,* which won two national awards, a state award and an U.S. Army-wide First Place Multi Media Award. In 2007, I produced, directed and edited another documentary for the Guard titled *Bataan, The Harrodsburg Tankers, A Time for Courage, A Time for Heroes,* winning a combined total of seven national and state awards, including a Telly Award in 2008 and the Award of Merit from the American Association of State and Local History in 2009. I was also presented the Medal of Merit from the Order of Saint Constantine in 2008 for the documentary. I also have produced several art prints of Civil War, Vietnam and Desert Storm soldiers.

I have continued to play drums since my time with Action Unlimited with several central Kentucky groups, including Showboat and The Classics. I currently play drums with an eight-piece horn group, Prime Cut, performing throughout the state of Kentucky. I married Anne Fallen, from Winchester, in 1973 and have three children, Jamie, Julie and Beth Pope. As of 2016, I am 70 years old, retired and living in Winchester.

Action Unlimited Reunion, 2003:

In 2003, Jeanne Lane sponsored a reunion for Action Unlimited, held in Gravel Switch, Kentucky. Four of the AU members made it to the reunion, with only Dave Osborn and Chuk Trisko, who had previous commitments, not making it. This was the first time the AU band members performed together on stage since 1967, when the group broke up in California. Vicki Jones Osborne and Marti Jones McGhee also performed on stage with AU as they were also in California with the group.

Performers at the Action Unlimited Reunion, 2003 at Gravel Switch, Kentucky. L-R: Vicki Jones Osborne, Sam McIntosh, Marti Jones McGhee, Dewey Pope, Jon Anderson and Kent Fox. Vicki and Marti performed as The Results and were on stage with Action Unlimited frequently during their careers.

About the Author

Winchester, Ky. native Dewey Pope is a 1964 graduate of George Rogers High School, where he focused on art and music. He played drums in several area bands, most notably Action Unlimited, with whom he toured until the band's breakup in 1967.

He served in the Army beginning in 1969 as an illustrator and entertainment specialist. Upon his discharge, he went to college, receiving a BA in Art in 1979. While working as a graphic artist and illustrator, he continued to satisfy his love of music by playing with several central Kentucky bands. He joined the Army Reserve in 1981, then the Kentucky Army National Guard in 1985, where he was Visual Information Manager. His work with the Guard earned Pope several awards for documentary production before his retirement in 2008.

He continues to keep his creative juices flowing by playing drums with the band Prime Cut, producing art prints and writing a book about his experiences in the '60s with Action Unlimited.

Index

A

Abney, Philip 16, 17
Anderson, Buddy 29, 47, 126
Anderson, Jon 6, 25, 29, 31, 33, 36, 39, 40, 43, 46, 54, 55, 60, 61, 68, 69, 70, 91, 93, 99, 100, 102, 107, 114, 116, 119, 126, 135, 136, 139, 145, 147, 148, 150, 151, 153, 154, 155, 159, 161, 162, 165, 166
Association, The 161

B

Bailey, Pearl 95
Barry, Len 86
Beach Boys, The 9, 29, 30, 72, 134, 150, 161
Beatles, The 8, 9, 56, 76
Becker, Bob 25, 99
Bellson, Louie 95, 96, 110
Boettcher, Curt 72, 81, 83, 161
Boone, Pat 134
Brown, James 60, 90, 157
Buffalo Springfield 50
Byrds, The 33, 72

C

Cameo-Parkway Records 86, 94, 129, 131, 140, 149, 153, 155
Campbell, Chuck 25, 99
Campbell, Glen 96
Cannon, Freddie 83
Carmichael, Hoagy 134, 150
Carousel Club, The 69
Chandler, Jim 135
Charles, Ray 76
Checker, Chubby 86
Checkmates, The 79
Clark, Dick 9, 27, 32, 36, 48, 59, 86, 161
Clark, Gene 72
Clark, Steve 71, 72, 73, 81, 82, 83, 86, 135, 140, 147, 149, 153, 155, 161
Cline, Johnny 13, 14
Coasters, The 50, 161
Colgan, Tom 25, 27, 40, 99
Collins, Gary 150
Columbia Studios 82, 83, 89, 131, 140
Cooke, Sam 76
Corbett, Glenn 151
Cornelison, Buzz 24, 98
Cotton, Neville 42
Crawford, Johnny 151
Crombie, Doug 93, 139, 142, 147, 149, 154, 157, 159

D

Davenport, Mack 24, 98
Davis, Richard 49
Dean, James 52
Demattia, Vince 51
DeSimone, Giovanni 135
Dick Clark's Caravan of Stars 27, 29, 32, 126
DiSimone, Giovanni 87, 150
Dovells, The 86
Dove, Ronnie 150
Drifters, The 23

E

Ecton, Bud 7, 13, 36, 95
Edwards, Gary 6, 24, 25, 26, 36, 39, 99, 161
Elton John 72

Evans, Wayne 158
Exile 7, 25
Exiles, The 9, 21, 23, 24, 98

F

Faith, Percy 82
Fallen, Anne 170
Fascinato, Jack 169
Ford, Tennessee Ernie 168
Four Seasons, The 50
Fox, Kent 6, 14, 17, 19, 27, 39, 41, 42, 54, 55, 56, 61, 65, 69, 70, 71, 72, 75, 76, 78, 79, 81, 88, 89, 91, 93, 95, 97, 100, 102, 115, 118, 121, 122, 123, 129, 130, 131, 145, 146, 157, 158, 159, 161, 168, 169
Fox, Peter Kevin 168
Fraley, Susan 168
Francis, Charlie 7
Fydallions, The 66, 67

G

Garner, James 134
Gary Edwards and The Embers 36
Gill, Gloria 169
Glenn Miller Orchestra 25
Greene, Lorne 51
Green, Karl 126

H

Harvey, Lawrence 134, 150
Head, Roy 50, 161
Herman's Hermits 27, 28, 29, 126, 161
Hilliard, Ronnie 20, 22
Howard, Mike 24, 98
Hullabaloo 83
Hutcherson, Jimmy "Hutch" 25, 99
Hyland, Brian 27, 161

I

Impressions, The 25, 99

J

Jacobs, George 134
James, Irene 129, 133, 134, 135, 150, 168, 169
Johnston, Bruce 134
Jones, Cecil 14, 41, 87
Jones, "Chip" 33
Jones, Frank 33
Jones, Marti 33, 34, 36, 47, 72, 88, 111, 171
Jones, Ruth 33
Jones, Tom 32, 161
Jones, Vicki 32, 34, 36, 47, 88, 111, 171
Joyce, Bill 14

K

Kaye, Harvey 67
Kincaid, Riley 32, 33, 36, 47, 48, 50, 51, 53, 54, 55, 57, 59, 60, 63, 66, 67, 68, 69, 71, 72, 73, 75, 76, 77, 78, 79, 81, 82, 83, 86, 88, 89, 93, 94, 95, 101, 129, 131, 136, 140, 141, 147, 149, 150, 153, 155, 157, 158, 159, 161, 162
Kincaid, Russ 47, 50, 96
Knickerbockers, The 49

L

Landon, Michael 51
Lane, Jeanne 39, 164, 171
Leaves, The 83
Leckenby, Derek 126
Lee, Rick 6
Linville, Ray 25, 99
Little Anthony and The Imperials 27, 161
Little Richard 76
Long, Richard 150
Lovin' Spoonful, The 50
Luxon, Billy 24, 98

M

Majors, Lee 150, 151
Mamas and the Papas, The 157
Margaret, Ann 51
Maroons, The 6, 8, 9, 21, 24, 25, 29, 32, 33, 39, 40, 41, 42, 99, 155, 165
Martin, Paul 7
McCannon, George III 59, 60, 161
McConkey, Gail 136
McIntosh, Lisa 7
McIntosh, Sam 7, 27, 34, 39, 40, 43, 54, 55, 61, 65, 69, 71, 82, 83, 84, 91, 93, 100, 102, 103, 112, 115, 130,

131, 135, 137, 142, 145, 149, 155, 159, 161, 166
Mercantile Records 168
Mercury Records 86
Mitchell, Denny 20
Mobley, Mary Ann 150
Monzzas, The 19, 20, 26, 27, 33, 34, 41, 42, 97, 158
Moore, John 25, 99
Morse, Jerry 27, 29, 33, 41, 100
Mostly Jeff 168
Mothers of Invention 9

N

Newbeats, The 77, 161
Nielson, Leslie 50
Noone, Peter "Herman" 28, 29, 126
Nooney Rickett Band, The 130

O

O'Connor, Donna 49
O'Neill, Jimmy 96, 161
Orbison, Roy 60
Orlons, The 86
Osborn, Dave 7, 25, 26, 31, 35, 39, 40, 43, 44, 54, 55, 59, 61, 69, 75, 79, 84, 85, 86, 89, 90, 91, 92, 93, 99, 100, 102, 103, 108, 120, 121, 130, 137, 139, 141, 142, 143, 145, 146, 147, 148, 149, 150, 151, 153, 154, 155, 158, 159, 161, 163, 164, 166, 171
Osborn, Jeanne 7, 35, 42

P

Parello, Vinny 67
Paul Revere and The Raiders 33, 72
Pearson, Ron 84
Pennington, J.P. 24
Pepper Swift and The Monzzas 22
Peter and Gordon 32, 161
Peter Moon 168
Peterson, Paul 49
Pickens, Slim 151
Pitney, Gene 150
Pope, Anne 6
Pope, Beth 171
Pope, Jamie 170
Pope, Julie 171
Presley, Elvis 49, 51
Preston, Billy 76, 77, 96, 161
Prime Cut 170, 172
Prine, Andrew 151

Q

Question Mark and the Mysterians 131

R

Rauth, Bill 25, 27, 99
Ray Anthony Orchestra 25
Red Velvet 115, 129
Red Velvet Club, The 48, 49, 51, 53, 54
Results, The 32, 33, 34, 36, 60, 62, 69, 72, 88, 111, 161, 171
Ridings, George 6, 25, 26, 99
Righteous Brothers, The 50
Ritchie, Danny 19
Rivers, Johnny 50
Roe, Tommy 33, 36, 71, 72, 81, 161
Rogers, Glen 16, 17
Rogers, Peggy 32, 33, 36
Ronnie and the Sensations 20
Ron Pearson and The Ron Dons 84
Royal, Billy Joe 29, 161
Russell, Leon 96
Rydell, Bobby 86

S

Sam the Sham and the Pharaohs 50
Sharp, Dee Dee 86
Showboat and The Classics 170
Sikes, Doug 7
Sinatra, Frank 134, 168
Sir Douglas Quintet 83, 161
Slucher, Kent 7
Slusher, Phil 25, 26, 27, 29
Smith, Paul 24
Smith, Paul Jr. 98
Smith, W.A. 15
Smokey Robinson and the Miracles 83
Speck's 7, 21, 23, 24, 26, 32, 33, 34, 146
Spencer, Gary 19, 97
Spicer, C.B. 14, 17, 19, 41, 42, 97
Spiral Starecase, The 66
Starks, John (Jabo) 157
Starr, Ringo 56
Stokley, Jimmy 23, 24, 98
Stoner, Pete 25, 26, 27

Stubblefield, Clyde 157
Swift, Pepper 20

T

Thomas, Jimmy 15, 16
Tom Petty and the Heartbreakers 129
Tony and the Bandits 29
Travis, William 134
Trip, The 48, 49, 50
Trisko, Chuk 6, 27, 29, 30, 32, 36, 39, 40, 43, 44, 50, 54, 55, 60, 61, 65, 69, 72, 75, 79, 81, 82, 88, 90, 91, 94, 100, 102, 103, 121, 122, 131, 136, 139, 145, 153, 154, 159, 161, 167, 168, 171
Trisko, David 168
True, Larry Joe 25, 26, 99
Turtles, The 32, 161
Tymes, The 86

U

Upton, Pat 67
Utmost, The 146

V

Vee, Bobby 27, 161

W

Walker, Jimmy 49
Wasson, Paul 15, 16, 19, 97, 158
Watkins, Hank 155, 157
Wayne, John 134
Weisinger, Larry 20
Welk, Lawrence 13, 14
Westbrook, Randy 7, 8
Whisky a Go-Go 50, 83
Whitwam, Barry 126
Williams, Ralph 69
Wilson, Brian 29
Wilson, Dennis 29, 150
Wilson, Ronnie 21
Wilson, Tommy 20, 21, 23
Wrecking Crew, The 81

Z

Zappa, Frank 72